SECRET UPPER PENINSULA

A GUIDE TO THE WEIRD, WONDERFUL, AND OBSCURE

Kath Usitalo

Reedy Press
PO Box 5131
St. Louis, MO 63139
www.reedypress.com

Library of Congress Control Number: 2019936712

ISBN: 9781681062235

All photos by author unless otherwise noted.

Insert photo credits: Adventure Mine Tours (page 90), Dummond Island Tourism (page 102), Edwin "Bill" Raisanen (pages 100–101), Little Traverse Conservatory (page 104), Ritch Branstrom (page 89), and Woods and Water (pages 96–97)

Design by Jill Halpin

Printed in the United States of America
21 23 24 5 4 3 2

DEDICATION

To Graham, whose innate curiosity and breadth of knowledge continue to amaze and inspire me.

CONTENTS

INTRODUCTION

There may be more things about Michigan's Upper Peninsula that are weird, wonderful, and obscure than there are bolts in the Mackinac Bridge (1,016,600). Or, at minimum, its miles of Great Lakes coastline (1,700). Don't tell anyone, but its quirkiness is a point of pride for many of the 306,000 Yoopers who call the UP home.

These secret stories just begin to scratch the surface of what's special about the UP, described by author Clarence A. Andrews as "a world unto itself, like the Old World of the nineteenth century." Whether you're comfy in your reading chair or on the road exploring, I hope this book reveals something new, surprising, and inspiring about the UP, which naturalist and photographer Edwin Way Teale called "that land of wonderful wilderness."

Welcome to da UP, you betcha!

Things to keep in mind as you travel the UP:

- Many businesses and attractions are seasonal, usually meaning sometime in May to sometime in October
- Bring some cash for those places that do not accept cards
- The UP has one area code (906) but two time zones; it's mostly Eastern, but along the Wisconsin border there's a zig-zag area on Central time
- Cell service can be spotty
- GPS is sometimes confused; pick up paper maps for back-up navigation
- Before exploring on backroads, be aware that some are better suited to SUVs and four-wheel drives than sedans
- Bugs live here; bring bug dope
- For visitor information consult the Upper Peninsula Travel and Recreation Association at uptravel.com and the state's Pure Michigan material at michigan.org
- Visit the staffed Michigan Welcome Centers for a good map, wealth of free information, and travel tips at Iron Mountain, Ironwood, Marquette, Menominee, St. Ignace, and Sault Ste. Marie. Michigan.gov/mdot

1 BEST LAID PLANS

Why was this military outpost active for only five of its twenty-six years?

Just beyond Copper Harbor, the tidy white buildings of Fort Wilkins gleam against the surrounding forest and deep blue water of Lake Fanny Hooe. Secretary of War William Wilkins ordered the stockade fort built in anticipation of trouble between the Indian population and the stream of men arriving in the Keweenaw Peninsula to work the copper mines. In 1844 two companies of the 5th Infantry Regiment arrived at the new garrison, but the 105 soldiers had little to do: no uprisings, no need for a military presence. In 1846 the troops were called to fight in the Mexican War, and the fort was abandoned. It wasn't used by the Army again until 1867, as a place for soldiers to serve out their entitlements. By 1870 Fort Wilkins was closed permanently, having served only five years of duty.

Reportedly, it was a destination for the Lake Superior Bicycle Club on outings in the 1880s and 1890s. In 1923 the fort became a Michigan state park, and in the 1930s restoration began as a WPA project. Most of the nineteen buildings are arranged in a U shape around the parade ground and include the kitchen and mess room, company quarters, officers' quarters, hospital, powder magazine, icehouse, storehouse, and bakery. Exhibits in the barracks, sutler store, married enlisted men's quarters, and hospital ward interpret what it would have been like to live in the remote fort.

The seven-hundred-acre state park has picnic tables, modern campgrounds, a foot trail, swimming, fishing, and more recreation options.

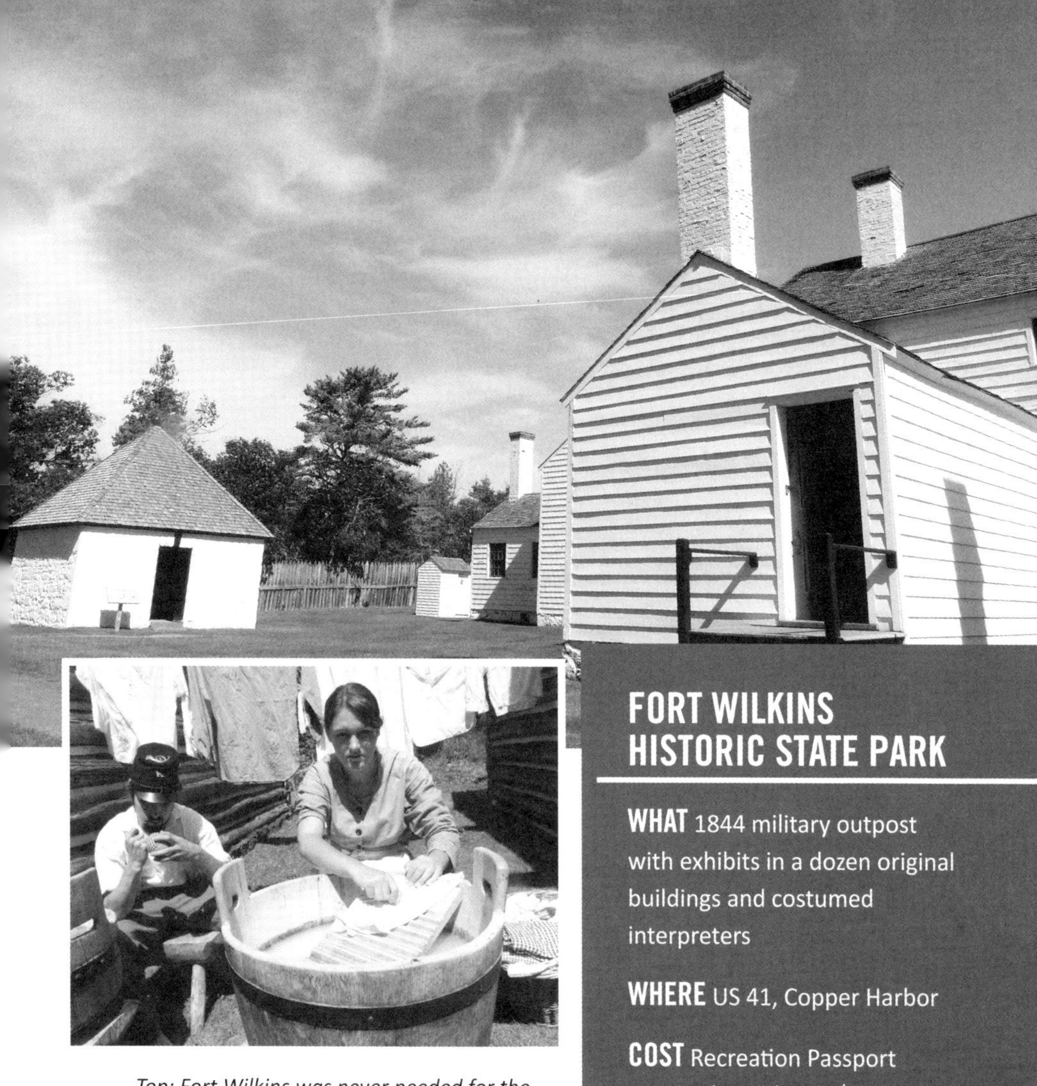

Top: *Fort Wilkins was never needed for the anticipated purpose of keeping law and order at the tip of the Keweenaw Peninsula.*

Inset: Perhaps not everyone was happy about being stationed at remote Fort Wilkins.

FORT WILKINS HISTORIC STATE PARK

WHAT 1844 military outpost with exhibits in a dozen original buildings and costumed interpreters

WHERE US 41, Copper Harbor

COST Recreation Passport required: residents, $12 annual; non-residents, $9 day pass, $34 annual

PRO TIP A two-day Civil War encampment takes place at the fort each July.

2 FRIENDLY GIANT

What city does the world's largest Indian call home?

On a sunny summer day in 1964, the people of Ironwood prepared for a very big event: the arrival of "the world's tallest and largest Indian." According to a report in the *Ironwood Daily Globe*, "Hundreds of people lined the streets, many of them with cameras, and gaped in awe at the sight before their eyes. The general comment heard that day was: 'I didn't think it would be that big.'"

The fifty-two-foot-tall fiberglass Hiawatha rolled into town on his back, strapped to a seventy-foot trailer that had to travel a circuitous, nearly fourteen-hour route from Minneapolis, where Gordon Displays constructed the colorful, nine-ton statue with an internal steel structure built to withstand 140 mph winds. The $10,000 roadside attraction was conceived by local car dealer Charles Gotta Sr. as a way to build the local tourism industry at the end of the once-prosperous iron mining era. "The Big Indian," as locals call him, stands in a triangular plot on the site of "Old Norrie," one of the six mines that had been productive from the 1880s until the last one closed in 1965.

Installation took place on Friday, June 26, following a parade led by the local saddle club and marching bands. Two steel support beams—one for each of Hiawatha's legs—had been sunk and secured in a foundation eight feet deep. An eighty-foot crane was required to lift Hiawatha and settle him onto the twenty-six-foot pillars, which entered through holes in the soles of his gigantic moccasins.

Hiawatha is the largest Indian statue by girth, but Maine's Skowhegan Indian is ten feet taller.

Hiawatha faces north, looking toward Gitche Gumee, Lake Superior.

HIAWATHA

WHAT The world's largest Indian

WHERE Hiawatha Park, bound by Burma Rd., E. Houk St., and Beech St., Ironwood

COST Free

PRO TIP Don't look for Hiawatha in an obvious spot on a busy roadway; he's at home in a tucked-away neighborhood park.

At the statue's fiftieth-anniversary celebration, the *Daily Globe* quoted local historian Larry Peterson, who explained Hiawatha's heritage. "He's representative of the Iroquois League, which is made up of five different tribes. What his extended hand means is a gesture of welcome. It's a gesture of peace."

3 MODEL TOWN

Where can you sleep in a tiny 1930s company town built by Henry Ford?

It looks like a movie set plunked down at the edge of the forested wilderness along US 41 in the western UP. Alberta Village's twelve tidy, Cape Cod-style homes line curved lanes, and a white, two-story sawmill anchors one end of the settlement. Shimmering across the highway, the twenty-acre Lake Plumbago exists because a creek was dammed to supply the steam-powered sawmill. The small community of Alberta was the vision of Henry Ford, an extension of the "Village Industries" he'd started in the 1920s in rural southeast Michigan. There, he set up small, hydroelectrically powered factories operated by local people who would maintain their farms while also producing automobile parts or packing the soybeans that Ford used to make paints and plastics. In the UP, he built his company towns around sawmills and logging operations.

At Alberta, eight miles south of L'Anse, the houses built for sawmill employees are named after trees: Spruce, Elm, Beech, Hemlock. But other than a school, there were none of the conveniences of daily living, such as stores, a church, or a post office. The sawmill operated from 1936 to 1954, and when

ALBERTA VILLAGE

WHAT One of Henry Ford's model towns, now owned by Michigan Tech and used in its forestry research

WHERE On US 41, eight miles south of L'Anse

COST Free to drive through; a few of the original homes are available for overnight stays beginning at $100 per night

PRO TIP Stop at Dave Stimac's Nature's Way Woodworking gallery and shop for household and decorative items and furniture handcrafted of birdseye maple.

The Alberta sawmill's first boards were used to construct the homes and buildings of Henry Ford's planned community.

the experiment ended, Alberta's buildings, Lake Plumbago and its dam, and 1,700 acres were donated to Michigan Tech University.

Don't call it a ghost town. All of the original structures are intact, and the compound has been in continuous use by the university's School of Forest Resources and Environmental Science for research and training as the Ford Center and Forest. Ford Center is available to groups for meetings and retreats, and some of the original village homes are rented to individuals for overnight stays. Plans are underway to refurbish and reopen the sawmill as a museum.

Visitors are welcome to paddle Lake Plumbago and hike to scenic Canyon Falls or follow the network of trails that crisscross the property.

4 A GLOWING CONCERN

Is it the lantern of a railroad man's ghost or swamp gas?

Sometimes it appears to be white, other times red or with a green aura. The beam glows steadily, but often it appears to be dancing. Or floating. The Paulding Light (aka Dog Meadow Light and spook light) has mystified and amused locals, attracted tourists and news crews, inspired paranormal investigations, and intrigued scientific minds looking for a rational explanation. The first known report of the mysterious light flickering in the Western UP forest was made by a group of teens in 1966. Soon, others witnessed the phenomenon. Word of the almost-nightly show spread, and so did the theories about its origin. Is it the lantern of a brakeman killed on the railroad tracks that supposedly ran through the valley? The beam of the ghost train itself? An elder looking for a lost child? Swamp gas? ET? Or the lights of distant highway traffic?

In 2010 a group of engineering Michigan Tech University students set out to study the situation, working on the distant

PAULDING LIGHT

WHAT A mysterious light that appears in the wilderness between the towns of Watersmeet and Paulding

WHERE Robbins Pond Rd. (Old US 45) off US 45, north of Watersmeet

COST Free

PRO TIP The viewing area can be tricky to find; ask locals for directions.

Even skeptics have been awed by the appearance of the light and its changing characteristics.

The source of the Paulding Light, visible on most nights, has been speculated about since first reported in 1966. Photo courtesy of Flivver99 at English Wikipedia.

headlights theory. Equipped with a spectrometer to measure light frequencies, a telescope, a video camera, and a prearranged pattern of signal lights, they concluded that the Paulding Light is nothing more than vehicle lights interacting with the atmosphere about seven miles away. Their explanation has been derided and dismissed by those who question why the light takes on so many shapes, sizes, colors, and patterns. And by those who just want to believe.

5 CLOUD 906

What is the UP definition of pure outdoor bliss?

Michigan's largest state park and only designated wilderness area stretches twenty-plus miles along the Lake Superior shoreline and occupies sixty thousand acres of the Western UP. More than half of that land is covered in old-growth forest recognized as a National Natural Landmark for being the "biggest and best tract of virgin Northern Hardwoods in North America." With its woods, waterfalls, lakes, streams, wildlife, and geological features, Porcupine Mountains Wilderness State Park (aka The Porkies) is national park material, and it may have been one if Michigan hadn't added it to its parks system in 1945.

Much of the beauty of The Porkies is accessible only on foot. The ninety miles of trails accommodate varying levels of ability, from a walk with a park ranger to learn about wolves to a two-mile trek to Union Spring (Michigan's second-largest natural bubbler after Kitch-iti-kipi), or tackling the rugged sixteen-mile Lake Superior Trail. The Escarpment Trail, a moderately difficult eight-mile loop, is rated one of the most scenic hikes for its views of Lake of the Clouds.

But one of the most breathtaking and photographed sights in the entire 906 area code is within easy reach at an ADA-accessible overlook. Lake of the Clouds, nestled between the park's namesake ridges in the valley three hundred feet below, can appear purple, pink, silver, or a range of blues, colored by the rising or setting sun, mood of the sky, reflection of passing clouds, rising mist, and settling fog. It's like being on Cloud 906.

One photographer, up before the crack of dawn to capture a serene Lake of the Clouds sunrise shot, found that there were at least sixty shutterbugs with the same idea.

The Lake of the Clouds overlook is an easily accessible spot for stunning photos at any time of year. Photo by William Cannon, U.S. Geological Survey.

LAKE OF THE CLOUDS

WHAT Photogenic lake nestled between ridges of Porcupine Mountains Wilderness State Park

WHERE 412 S. Boundary Rd. via M-107, Ontonagon

COST Recreation Passport required: residents, $12 annual; non-residents, $9 day pass, $34 annual

PRO TIP Go to the overlook at night and catch a dark sky show on your own, or check the park schedule for a ranger-hosted star watch with telescope.

6 GET TO THE POINT

It's the picture of secluded splendor, with a dramatic, rocky shoreline, spectacular views, and crystal clear water, so what's the fly in the ointment?

North of the village of L'Anse, a slender finger of forested land juts into Lake Superior, the remote and wildly beautiful Point Abbaye at its tip. Huron Bay laps at the eastern shore and Keweenaw Bay the west side of the twelve-plus-mile Abbaye Peninsula. At its base is Pequaming, the ghost of a company town that boomed in the late 1800s with the region's first major lumbering and milling operation. In 1923, Henry Ford purchased the settlement and forty thousand acres to supply material for his vehicles' wooden floorboards, parts, and paneling. He developed Pequaming into his vision of a model town, and the community survived until the mid-1940s—but that's another story.

It's a slow go along the eleven or so miles of Point Abbaye Road as it winds through mostly state forest land to the rustic 260-acre Baraga County park (think outhouse). A short walk from the parking area leads to a breathtaking, panoramic view of the Huron Mountains, Huron Islands, and Keweenaw Peninsula. The remote park has two miles of rugged shore and impressive slabs of rock. There's no sandy beach; those brave enough have to jump off the massive boulders into Lake Superior's chilly water.

Adjacent to Point Abbaye, the thirty-acre Finlander Bay Nature Area, protected by the Keweenaw Land Trust, has rustic camping sites on a free, first-come, first-served basis.

Jumpers brave the biting flies and Lake Superior's cold water at Point Abbaye.

Gradual improvements to the county park will continue to draw more visitors, but it's remote enough to deter the crowds. Of course, the flies may stop some people, especially in the height of summer. These black, biting flies are not a mere nuisance; they are vicious and relentless with their sharp, stabbing attacks. Dozens will coat clothing and bite through layers—even jeans. But the pests are not there every day. If the breeze is right and the flies are absent, this tranquil wilderness park is worth the drive.

POINT ABBAYE

WHAT Baraga County park at Point Abbaye

WHERE 25 miles northeast of the village of L'Anse on the Abbaye Peninsula

COST Free

PRO TIP Gas up the vehicle, bring bug dope, water, food—the necessities.

7 EXTREME DETOUR

In what city did 230 brand-new automobiles get stranded due to an intense winter storm?

The blizzard that wrapped around the Keweenaw Peninsula on November 30, 1926, brought more ashore than heavy winds and blinding snow. The *City of Bangor*, a 445-foot cargo freighter turned automobile carrier, was loaded with 248 new Chrysler 50 and Whippet cars en route from Detroit to Duluth, Minnesota, when her steering power failed in a Lake Superior storm. Massive waves relentlessly pounded the deck, washing eighteen of the Chryslers into the raging waters. With the *Bangor* smashed against the rocky shore, her engines flooded and icing over, Captain W. J. Mackin and his crew of twenty-eight made their way to land and tried to keep from freezing, in clothing ill-suited for the elements.

All hands were rescued by the US Coast Guard, and attention turned to the challenge of retrieving the 230 vehicles aboard the *Bangor*. When the lake froze around the vessel, workers constructed a ramp of ice and snow so that the cars—safe and dry in the hold, separated from the flooded engine room—could be driven off the ship. Those on the top deck were encased in ice several feet thick and had to be carefully chipped free. They were parked in remote Copper Harbor for months before a road could be cleared through the deep snow so that dozens of local men and boys—paid five dollars each—could drive

CITY OF BANGOR

WHAT Museum exhibit about a freighter stranded in 1926 and the rescue of her crew and 230 new cars bound for Duluth from Detroit

WHERE M-26, Eagle Harbor

COST $5; children, free

PRO TIP Get the most from your admission fee and allow time to explore the four museums of the Eagle Harbor Lighthouse Complex.

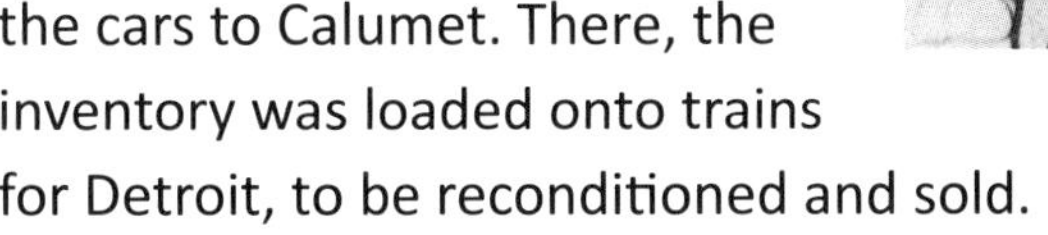

Left: The Chrysler 50 on display in Eagle Harbor may or may not have prematurely rolled off the City of Bangor *near Keweenaw Point.*

Right: The parade of Chryslers rescued from the City of Bangor. *Photo courtesy of Keweenaw National Historical Park Service.*

the cars to Calumet. There, the inventory was loaded onto trains for Detroit, to be reconditioned and sold.

The Keweenaw History Museum's *City of Bangor* exhibit features a Chrysler 50 purported to be one of those that survived the 1926 ordeal. How did it miss the train to Detroit? Was it washed ashore in the spring thaw? Did its driver take a "wrong turn" on his way to Calumet? With vehicle records destroyed in a fire, its provenance remains a secret.

The remains of the *City of Bangor* are protected by the Keweenaw Underwater Preserve, but the wreck was scrapped on site in 1942, and divers find little more than scattered pieces of it on the floor of Lake Superior.

8 CHRISTMAS EVE TRAGEDY

What is the terrible event memorialized in folk singer Woody Guthrie's song "1913 Massacre"?

Calumet, known as Red Jacket until 1929, was the largest city in the booming Copper Country, where the Calumet and Hecla Mining Company was the industry's major employer. By 1913, an organized labor push came to the region, and in July the Western Federation of Miners (WFM) called for a strike of all the region's mines. In addition to safer working conditions and higher wages, the union demanded a reduction of the typical twelve-hour workday to eight hours. By December the bitter strike had ground on for five months, with no agreement in sight.

A women's group affiliated with the WFM organized a Christmas Eve party for the families of striking miners, and hundreds of people attended the celebration at the Italian Benevolent Society building in downtown Calumet. As the afternoon festivities went on in the second-floor hall, someone falsely cried "Fire!" and panic ensued. In the stampede for the only stairway leading to the exit, people were tripped, trampled, and smothered in the crush. After the chaos cleared, seventy-three had died—fifty-nine of them children—in what is known as the Italian Hall

ITALIAN HALL DISASTER

WHAT Memorial park at the site of the social center where seventy-three died in Calumet's 1913 Christmas Eve catastrophe

WHERE Seventh and Elm Sts., Calumet

COST Free

PRO TIP Also in Calumet, the Keweenaw National Historical Park Visitor Center has a few artifacts and a three-minute film about the tragedy; doors from the Italian Hall are preserved at the Copper Country Firefighters History Museum.

The sandstone arch is all that remains of Calumet's Italian Hall, which was built in 1908 and demolished in 1984. Photo by Joanne Thomas.

Disaster. Some twenty thousand people flocked to Calumet for the mass funeral procession on December 28.

In the aftermath, accusations were made and multiple witnesses swore that it was an antiunion person who made the false call, but after an investigation, no one was charged in the incident. In April of 1914 miners ended the strike. For many, the resentment and suspicions over what was called a massacre lasted for generations. When the Italian Hall was razed in 1984, the archway of the main entrance was saved and stands as a memorial in a small park at the location.

A group of volunteers raised funds for the granite Italian Hall Tragedy Victims Memorial engraved with the names of the seventy-three who died.

9 PEAK EXPERIENCE

Where do you go to reach the pinnacle of Michigan?

On the list of highest natural points in every state in the United States, Michigan's Mt. Arvon comes in at number thirty-eight, between those of Minnesota and Wisconsin. Located in the Huron Mountains of the Western UP, Mt. Arvon peaks out at 1,979.238 feet above sea level. Its distinction as the state's high point came relatively recently. Until 1982 the honor belonged to nearby Mt. Curwood, which is named for James Oliver Curwood, a conservationist and popular Michigan adventure writer of the 1920s and 1930s. Then, a survey team found that Mt. Arvon had Curwood beat by a mere foot.

The Weyerhaeuser timber company owns Mt. Arvon, and the property is, naturally, crisscrossed with old logging roads. There have been recent improvements to the route to the top, but the last two miles can be challenging. (Directions are complicated; stop by the Baraga County tourism office or check baragacounty.org for instructions.) A hiking trail makes for a nice alternative route to the summit. Once you've arrived through a recently cleared opening in the forest, you can see a bazillion trees—and on a clear day, the Keweenaw Peninsula and Lake Superior.

After you've made it to the top of Mt. Arvon, stop at the Baraga County tourism office for a certificate that verifies your accomplishment.

A distant view of Lake Superior, about ten miles north of Mt. Arvon. Photo courtesy of Baraga County Tourism.

MT. ARVON

WHAT Michigan's highest natural point

WHERE A 27-mile drive east of L'Anse

COST Free

PRO TIP Depending on the weather, parts of the road can be rough, muddy, and better tackled in a 4WD vehicle; access is by snowshoes or snowmobile in winter.

10 HIGH-FLYING FEELING

How do you get to the top of North America's only ski jump if you're not a ski jumper?

There are just five international ski flying sites in the world, and one of them is in the Western UP. And it happens to be the largest ski jump structure built on the top of a hill, which means that the top of Copper Peak is very, very high up there—as in 1,180 feet above Lake Superior, which, by the way, is visible from that height. The view also takes in 2,500 square miles of scenic beauty over three states and, on a clear day, Canada. Copper Peak ski jump opened in 1970 and hosted ski flying competitions (albeit not many) into the early 1990s. It now operates as the Copper Peak Adventure Ride, which is how you can satisfy your inner ski jumper.

First, you take an 810-foot chairlift ride to the crest of the hill, where an elevator whisks you upwards for eighteen stories, to the main observation platform. If you're not satisfied with that scenery, you have the option of climbing another eight floors to the ski flyers' starting gate at the peak of the Peak, where a forty-mile view unfolds. The fall colors from twenty-six stories up are spectacular.

Efforts are underway to bring Copper Peak facilities up to date and equipped to host summertime ski jumping competitions.

From Copper Peak you can take in a forty-mile view of the Western UP, Lake Superior, and even Canada. Photo by Brad Nelson.

COPPER PEAK ADVENTURE RIDE

WHAT Go to the top of the largest artificial ski jump in the world.

WHERE N 13870 Copper Peak Rd., Ironwood

COST Adults, $22; youth, $8; under five, free

PRO TIP Don't panic if you feel you're swaying in the breeze; the ski jump is designed to fluctuate up to eighteen inches and withstand winds of 190 mph.

11 SHE LOVES YOU TRULY

How did a Michigan widow become the first female superstar songwriter?

Carrie Jacobs-Bond was born in Janesville, Wisconsin, in 1862, and from the age of four she showed a knack for music, picking out tunes on the piano. After a short marriage that produced her only child, Frederick, she divorced her first husband. In 1889 she married Frank Lewis Bond, who moved the family to Iron River, where he worked as the iron mine doctor. He encouraged her to start writing music, and in 1894 her first songs, "Is My Dolly Dead?" and "Mother's Cradle Song," were published.

With mines closing, Dr. Bond became unemployed, and due to his bad investments and death in 1895, the family faced financial difficulty. The widow and her son left Iron River for

CARRIE JACOBS-BOND HOME

WHAT Indoor/outdoor Iron County Historical Museum

WHERE 100 Brady Ave., Caspian

COST Adults, $10; youth, $5; under five, free; family ticket, $25

PRO TIP Plan to spend some time exploring the many buildings on the grounds and the museum exhibits, including the work of local lad Lee LeBlanc, who left for Hollywood and worked as an animator and MGM art director from 1937 to 1962. He returned to Iron River and became an award-winning wildlife artist.

The museum's collection of log structures earned it the designation of the "Historic Log Cabin Capital of Michigan."

Carrie Jacobs-Bond said she spent some of the happiest years of her life in this house in the UP.

Janesville, where she wrote what would become her most famous piece, "I Love You Truly." From there she moved to Chicago to pursue her music writing and publishing career and sold a million copies of the popular parlor song. That tune, "Just a Wearyin' for You," and "The End of a Perfect Day" were the most lasting of the more than 175 compositions she published.

The Bond home was relocated from Iron River to the grounds of the Iron County Historical Museum in nearby Caspian, where it is partially furnished with the composer's belongings. Jacobs-Bond built a music publishing empire and was twice invited to the White House, but she suffered ill health and many personal tragedies. She said, "I spent my seven happiest years in Iron River, Michigan."

12 COPPER COUNTRY DREAMING

How are two engineers bringing the copper era back to life, one Victorian home at a time?

Copper built Calumet, the center of the booming industry from the mid-1800s until the mid-1960s. Cruising the quiet business district today, it's hard to picture downtown Calumet bustling with a turn-of-the-last-century population of four thousand (plus twenty-five thousand in adjoining mining towns). Back then, Vertin Bros. Department Store carried everything from home goods to the latest in ladies' fashions. The Calumet Theatre attracted luminaries like Lillian Russell, Douglas Fairbanks Sr., and John Philip Sousa. While miners earned twenty-five cents an hour, mining executives, store owners, and other successful businessmen put their wealth into grand homes. Thanks to Julie and David Sprenger, it's possible to imagine the opulence of the era as a guest at stately homes that, over the last thirty years, they have transformed into boutique hotels.

The couple met as Michigan Tech University students, who, after graduation, moved to California, where they put their engineering degrees to work while also buying, renovating, and flipping properties. It was something they were good at and enjoyed, and in 1989 they moved back to the UP and returned a derelict, thirteen-thousand-square-foot mansion to its former glory as Laurium Manor Inn, a boutique hotel. The forty-five-room Neoclassical-style home was built in 1908 by Thomas Hoatson, owner of the Calumet and Arizona Mining Company. His $50,000 bought the silver-leaf music room ceiling and the wall covering of embossed, gilded elephant hide in the dining room, where breakfast is served to guests of the inn's eleven rooms. The Sprengers then transformed the thirty-four-room home across the street, which was built in

Left: *Julie and David Sprenger have been restoring homes as guest lodging since 1989.*

Right:The thirteen-thousand-square-foot home of a copper baron welcomes overnight guests as the Laurium Manor Inn.

LAURIUM MANOR INN

WHAT The first of the homes from the wealthy copper era that have been renovated by Julie and David Sprenger as boutique lodging

WHERE 320 Tamarack St., Laurium

COST $119 per night and up

PRO TIP Be aware of the stairs. Guest rooms are on the second and third floors of these historic homes, and there are no elevators.

1906 by a drugstore owner, into Victorian Hall B&B. Incredibly, the two continue to save historic properties in their neighborhood. After decades of renovating properties together, Julie laughs, "We are still married, and even still like each other."

In addition to the two mansions, the Sprengers have updated three comparatively modest homes in the neighborhood as weekly vacation rentals.

13 FROZEN IN TIME

Where can you step into the self-sufficient farm life of an immigrant family of the 1920s?

The story of Herman Hanka and his family is more typical of the nineteenth-century immigration experience than it is extraordinary. But it is a story remarkably told at their home, a humble subsistence farm carved out of the forest, miles from anywhere, where they lived from 1896 until the last son died in 1966. Preserved by dedicated volunteers as the Hanka Homestead Finnish Museum, it allows a peek into the past and into life as it was for this self-reliant family.

Herman Hanka, his wife, Wilhelmina, and their children came to America from Finland in the 1880s and made their way to Calumet, where he worked as a driller in the copper mines. The dangerous job required drilling holes into rock walls and stuffing the holes with blasting powder, which was detonated to break up the rock to get to the copper. An explosion that killed his partner left Hanka deaf and disabled, and so the family returned to farming—they had been tenant farmers in Finland. They first homesteaded a 160-acre farm and then moved to eighty acres near the base of the Keweenaw Peninsula, in the area known as Askel Hill. With the Finnish resolve known as *sisu*, they built the house, sauna, multiple barns, sheds, and other outbuildings. They grew

---

The homestead didn't change much after the 1920s. It's a rare example of a historical, working-class farm, with structures in their original locations, filled with the family's possessions.

Volunteers have restored and maintain the original, hand-hewn log structures at Hanka Homestead. Photo by Edwin "Bill" Raisanen.

and canned vegetables, made hay, harvested firewood, fished, hunted and trapped game, kept chickens and cows, baked and made butter, forged tools—in short, they did whatever they needed to do to survive.

HANKA HOMESTEAD FINNISH MUSEUM

WHAT The hand-hewn log buildings of the immigrant family who lived on the farm from the 1890s to 1966

WHERE 13249 Hanka Rd., Baraga. About 10 miles north of Baraga on US 41, turn west onto Arnheim Rd; at the fire tower follow the gravel road to the farm road

COST $4 suggested donation

PRO TIP Interpretive and self-guided tours are available. See demonstrations of home and farm skills, enjoy folk music, and more at Heritage Day each August.

14 LOST LADY FOUND

Why is there a bent airplane propeller in front of the Lake Linden village hall?

A World War II tragedy is memorialized in Lake Linden, the hometown of USAAF Technical Sgt. Robert E. LaMotte. On April 4, 1943, *Lady Be Good*, a B-24D Liberator, was one of twenty-five aircraft on a two-part bombing raid of Naples, Italy. Due to a sandstorm and issues with the other aircraft, *Lady* headed back solo to the base in Libya. The pilot, 1st Lt. William J. Hatton, radioed that the aircraft's navigation equipment wasn't working. *Lady* and her crew, including radio operator LaMotte, weren't heard from again. The USAAF concluded that *Lady* and her crew of nine had gone down in the Mediterranean Sea.

Flash forward to November of 1958, when a British oil exploration team flying over the Libyan Desert spotted wreckage. In May of 1959—sixteen years after the crash—a recovery team confirmed that it was the long-lost *Lady Be Good*. She had not crashed in the sea, but skidded to a rough landing in the desert. Although in pieces, *Lady* was in relatively good shape; amazingly, the radio was still in working condition. Between February and August of 1960 the remains of eight, including LaMotte, were recovered from the desert.

LADY BE GOOD TRIBUTE

WHAT A bent propeller from the lost American B-24D Liberator that went down in the Libyan Desert in April of 1943 honors the crew, including local Robert E. LaMotte

WHERE 401 Calumet St., Lake Linden

COST Free

PRO TIP Cross the street and treat yourself to ice cream or a meal at Lindell Chocolate Shoppe, a local institution since 1922.

Left: One of four three-bladed propellers from the ill-fated Lady Be Good *honors the lost crew, including Lake Linden local Robert E. LaMotte. Photo by Dan Reynard.*

Right: US Army veteran Dan Reynard photographed the Lady Be Good *monument on a "Tour of Honor" that he made in honor of fellow military. Photo by Dan Reynard.*

A diary kept by copilot 2nd Lt. Robert F. Toner helped to piece together the story. Running low on fuel, the disoriented crew—thinking they were over water—parachuted from the plane. Separated from the wreck and one of their own, the eight survivors set off on foot. It was a torturous journey through scorching hot days and frigid nights, with only a few rations and a half-canteen of water to share. After walking about eighty miles, five of the men could not go on and the others continued the trek. It appears that by April 13, 1943, all had perished.

The Arnold Air Society at Michigan Tech University named its squadron after LaMotte, and each year its members clean and care for the *Lady Be Good* monument.

15 BIG MAN ON CAMPUS

Where will you find a tribute to the world's tallest-known justice of the peace?

The City of Hancock, in the Keweenaw Peninsula, shows the deep influence of immigrants from Finland in its Finnish street signs, diners serving Finnish foods, annual Finnish-themed festivals and the private Finlandia University, which was founded in 1896 as Suomi College.

One of the immigrant families, headed by Lauri and Annie Moilanen, traveled from Finland to Hancock in 1889 when their son, also named Lauri, was four years old. Dad was of average build and mom reportedly stood about four feet tall; of their four children, only Lauri (aka Louie) grew to a stupendous size. By the age of eighteen he stood more than eight feet tall. He wore size nineteen shoes and was, for a time, declared the tallest man in the world.

After working on the family farm, Louie got a job in the local copper mine. Although he could do the work of two men, his size hampered his career in the cramped environment. For a couple of years he toured with a circus but tired of the attention. He returned to Hancock and became a justice of the peace, and in 1913 he died at the age of twenty-seven.

BIG LOUIE MONUMENT

WHAT See how you measure up to the once-world's tallest man at the marker the height of the man it honors.

WHERE Next to the Finnish American Heritage Center at 435 Quincy St., Hancock

COST Free

PRO TIP Pop into the Finnish American Heritage Center and check out what art exhibit or event is happening and browse the goods at North Wind Books.

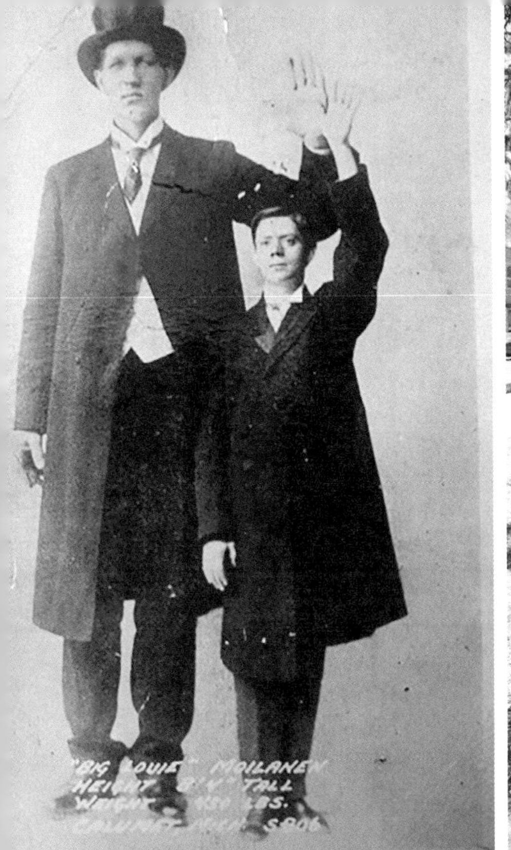

The monument stands as tall as Big Louie, at eight feet three inches; his parents and siblings were all of average size. Monument photo by David Maki. Historical photo credit Finnish American Heritage Center.

Louie is interred in his nine-foot-by-three-foot coffin at Lakeside Cemetery, west of Hancock, where his grave marker declares he weighed 560 pounds and stood eight feet three inches tall.

That is the height of the marker created a century after his death and installed on the Finlandia University campus, a monumental tribute to the “Giant Finn of the Copper Country.”

The Hancock community rallied to raise the funds for the monument, a 3,500-pound block of black granite with the memorial message in both Finnish and English.

16 CULTURAL PHENOMENON

What former church went from horror movie set to cultural center?

With the copper boom that began the 1840s, the Keweenaw Peninsula's mines were a magnet for workers from Canada and a multitude of European countries. At the heart of the activity was Calumet, where each ethnic group—the Cornish, Scots, Italians, Finns, Swedes, Croatians, Slovenians, and French Canadians—had its own church. As mining operations slowed, the populations dwindled; by the mid-1960s the copper era was over. Many of the churches still stand; some are active, and others have been repurposed, including the former St. Anne's, which was completed in 1901 for the French Canadian Catholic congregation. The soaring structure was constructed of Jacobsville Sandstone in a dramatic Gothic style and could accommodate eight hundred for mass—more than enough room for the entire population of Calumet today.

KEWEENAW HERITAGE CENTER

WHAT Splendid former St. Anne's Church transformed into a cultural and activity center

WHERE 25725 Scott St., Calumet

COST By donation

PRO TIP Check the schedule for Musical Monday performers.

After the church was deconsecrated in 1966, a private buyer turned it into a flea market and allowed it to be used for filming the 1991 cult horror movie *Children of the Night*. A few years

---

At one time there were six Catholic churches in Calumet, plus the Protestant and Jewish places of worship.

St. Anne's Catholic Church was deconsecrated in 1966 and is now the Keweenaw Heritage Center.

later a group of local citizens organized its rescue, and through their fundraising and volunteer efforts have restored the long-neglected building and transformed it into the Keweenaw Heritage Center. While the altar and pews have been removed, the beautiful stained glass windows and decorative interior details remain. In the large hall, the center focuses on preserving and interpreting the social aspects of life in the mining community through summertime exhibits, speaker programs, and concerts, including performances on a restored circa-1898 Barckhoff Tracker organ that came from a Lutheran church in Calumet.

17 HIDDEN TREASURE

Where's the gold in them thar hills?

Douglass Houghton, Michigan's first geologist, was responsible for mapping and appraising the state's natural resources for the State Geological Survey. In his 1841 report to the state legislature, he wrote extensively about the copper he found in the UP and spurred the nation's first mineral rush with his assessment that "the copper ores are not only of superior quality, but also that their associations are such as to render them easily reduced."

Houghton was also the first to go on record as having discovered gold in the UP. While on an expedition in 1845 to what is now Negaunee, he found the metal and took enough of a sample "to fill an eagle's quill." Not wanting the rest of his survey team to catch gold fever, Houghton kept the discovery to himself, later sharing it with one trusted associate. Unfortunately, he never revealed the exact location of the potential lode and later that year took the secret to his grave. In October, while on another survey along

DOUGLASS HOUGHTON MONUMENT

WHAT Small memorial to a big figure in the exploration of the UP

WHERE On M-26, Eagle River

COST Free

PRO TIP If one is good, two are better: there is a second Houghton tribute, a state historical marker, on Fourth Street in Eagle River.

Subsequent to Houghton's discovery, pure gold and electrum, a natural gold-silver alloy, were found across the state, but nothing to compare with the bountiful red metal of Copper Country.

The memorial to State Geologist Douglass Houghton was built of rocks from UP copper and iron mines and dedicated in 1914.

Lake Superior near Eagle River, he and two associates drowned when their small boat capsized in a storm. Houghton was buried in Detroit, where he lived with his wife and daughter, but he's not forgotten in the Keweenaw Peninsula. Among other things, the city of Houghton, Houghton County, and Douglass Houghton Falls are named for him, and the Keweenaw Historical Society dedicated a memorial in his honor in Eagle River. Fittingly, it is composed of rocks from UP copper and iron mines.

18 BRAKE FOR A BREAK

Where is the location of the first roadside park in the country?

It's only fitting that the state that put the world on wheels is the home of the first roadside park. Or rather, as the Michigan state historical marker at Larson Roadside Park in the Western UP hedges, "quite likely America's first such facility."

The Model T Ford had been in production for ten years when Herbert F. Larson, an engineer and manager of the Iron County highway department, saw a need for the growing number of automobile travelers to have a place to take a break from the road. In 1918 Larson convinced the county to preserve a 320-acre parcel of forested land along US 2, about four miles east of the city of Iron River, as a tourist rest area. The following year a picnic table was added, and the roadside park was born. In the 1920s, the concept took off across the country.

Michigan also declares—with a second state historical marker in the Lower Peninsula—to be the home of the first roadside table, which an employee built of scrapped wood and placed at a site in Ionia County in 1929. The Michigan Department of Transportation operates several categories of rest stops, so both "first" claims can be rationalized.

Michigan has more than eighty roadside parks, seventy-seven modern rest areas, nearly forty table sites, and some two dozen scenic turnouts.

UP highway engineer Herbert Larson is credited with creating the first roadside park.

FIRST ROADSIDE PARK

WHAT A shady spot to rest, revive, and take a break from the road

WHERE Four miles east of Iron River on US 2

COST Free

PRO TIP Pack a picnic and enjoy the company of towering old-growth trees.

19 GHOST BUSTERS

Who are the people that bring a UP ghost town to life each July?

Ghost towns dot the UP. They are shadows of company towns that died out when the lumber or minerals were depleted, or industry moved on, or farms failed. Some stand as a cluster of abandoned buildings at a crossroads; others are nothing more than the rubble of foundations. A handful are preserved as historical sites open to the public as museums. Central, in the upper reaches of the Keweenaw Peninsula, is one of those—a copper town that sprang up when the mining operation began in 1854 and faded after the reason for its being closed in 1898.

A cluster of buildings survives at Central (also called Central Mine) and are being restored by the Keweenaw County Historical Society. One serves as a visitor center with exhibits about life and work in the community that once topped 1,200; two restored miners' homes are also open to the public. Central's largely Cornish population built its first permanent church in 1868; the building still stands and is privately owned and maintained. Just one day each year, on the fourth Sunday of July, the church opens its doors to carry on a tradition that began in 1907, when nostalgic, displaced Central Mine families held a reunion. More than a century later, their descendants come together to worship and honor their heritage.

CENTRAL

WHAT A productive copper-mining town for forty-four years, now a ghost town you can tour

WHERE US 41, five miles east of Phoenix

COST Free; donations accepted

PRO TIP The annual reunion church services are open to all.

Stroll at your own pace through the remaining buildings of the one-time boomtown of Central Mine.

You can stay for a week in a miner's home that has been restored and updated as a Wi-Fi- and TV-free visitor rental. Proceeds benefit the historical society's restoration efforts.

20 LEGENDARY LIDS

How are Yoopers taking the hat world by storm?

If not for Bob Jacquart, the sturdy, six-panel Stormy Kromer cap that has sheltered heads since Theodore Roosevelt was president might not have seen its one-hundredth anniversary. The hat was created in 1903 by the wife of Wisconsin railroad engineer George "Stormy" Kromer, who was tired of losing his baseball caps aboard the windy trains. Ida adapted the former ballplayer's favorite style of headgear, adding a pull-down earband so that it fit snugly and securely. The practical lid caught on with other workers, Kromer patented the distinctive design, and sales flourished.

In 2001 Ironwood businessman Jacquart learned that the maker of the hats was floundering. Its demise would have devastated the workers, hunters, farmers, and outdoorsmen who depended on the utilitarian caps to keep their craniums warm and dry. Within a month, Jacquart purchased and relocated the business from Milwaukee to his fabric products facility in Ironwood. Bob's father, Robert Sr., had started the company in 1958 by making bank deposit bags; over the decades it grew to include stitching custom boat covers and upholstery and producing orthopedic pillows, gun cases, pet beds, and more—including fleece hats.

Since becoming a Jacquart Fabric Products company, Stormy Kromer's growth has exploded from production of a mere 3,800 hats in 2001 to more than 100,000 a year. Its appeal

---

The story of the Kromer hat is told in the 1965 children's Little Golden Book *Mr. Puffer-Bill: Train Engineer.*

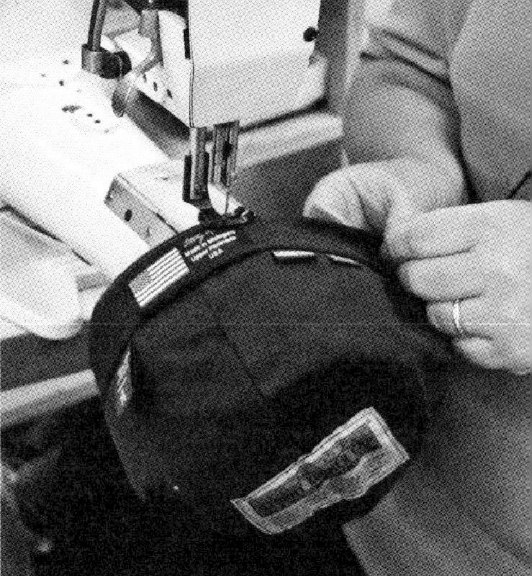

Left: Cap off your visit to Ironwood with a Stormy Kromer photo op.

Right: Each Stormy Kromer hat is made of multiple pieces and is hand sewn and hand inspected.

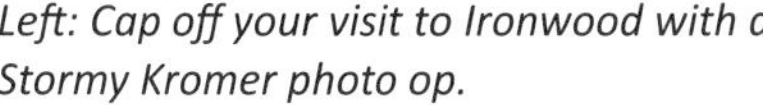

STORMY KROMER FACTORY TOUR

WHAT See the iconic caps being made by hand on a guided tour, Monday–Friday at 1:30 p.m. CST.

WHERE 1238 Wall St., Ironwood

COST Free, plus shopping allowance

PRO TIP Take a photo with the giant Stormy cap on the south side of US 2 at Luxmore St., not far from the factory.

reaches beyond its rural roots, from Brooklyn to Hollywood, with an expanded product line of hats, apparel, and accessories that includes women's and children's wear and pet gear. Stormy Kromer continues to grow, with Jacquart's daughters KJ Jacquart and Gina Jacquart Thorsen, who is the company president, carrying on the work started by Ida Kromer in 1903. Free factory tours end in the retail store.

21 LABOR OF LOVE

To what lengths did a young man go to win the hand of the girl he loved?

In 1886 Finnish immigrants who came to the Keweenaw Bay community of Jacobsville to work in the red sandstone quarries formed a Lutheran congregation, but they didn't have a home church building. One of those young men, Leander Sinko, fell in love with Maria Niemi, another Finnish immigrant. When he proposed marriage, his intended bride announced, "I want to be married in church." The earnest young man promised, "I'll build one."

In 1888 Sinko completed construction of a simple, wooden chapel in the woods, and on December 22, 1889, the couple married in the church's first wedding ceremony. A stone foundation was built in 1891, and the following year the bell tower was added to the front of the church. Since 1952 it has been a part of Gloria Dei Lutheran Church of Hancock, but little else has changed. The structure has no electricity or plumbing; it still retains the original furnishings, kerosene chandelier, woodstove, and pump organ. The chapel hosts Sunday evening vespers services in the summer and wedding ceremonies throughout the warm weather months.

Dr. J. K. Nikander, who presided over the Sinko-Niemi wedding, founded the Suomi College and Theological Seminary in 1896 in Hancock (now Finlandia University).

Visitors are welcome at summer vespers in the Finnish Lutheran chapel, which looks much as it did in the 1890s.

JACOBSVILLE LUTHERAN CHAPEL

WHAT Historic Finnish Evangelical Lutheran Church of Jacobsville

WHERE Red Rock Rd., Lake Linden

COST Free

PRO TIP People of all faiths are welcome to attend vespers services at 7 p.m. on Sundays from June through August.

22 HOCKEYVILLE USA

Where can you see a hockey game at the oldest indoor ice arena in the world?

Hockey is a way of life in the Copper Country. Houghton, the gateway to the Keweenaw Peninsula, is recognized as the birthplace of professional hockey. Just a dozen miles up the road, the Calumet Colosseum qualifies as the oldest in-use indoor ice arena in the world. Built in 1913, the old barn retains its distinctive style and classic appeal, with its three-story-high barrel roof, curved ceiling, grid of rafters, and simple bench seating for 990. The windows had to be opened to let the winter cold in to keep the rink, built with a single sheet of natural ice, in shape.

The Colosseum did upgrade to artificial ice in 1968, with most of the work done in record time by a volunteer force of striking copper miners. Long-overdue improvements are happening with the $150,000 prize that comes with being named Kraft Hockeyville USA 2019, thanks to the spirited community that rallied the most votes in the online competition.

CALUMET COLOSSEUM

WHAT Classic ice arena and community center for more than a century

WHERE 110 Red Jacket Rd., Calumet

COST Free to check out the lobby exhibits; fees vary for events

PRO TIP Locals have their favorite seats, so respect their space if you find spots staked out.

The International Frisbee and USA Guts Hall of Fame is housed on the Colosseum's second floor; in 1958, the first Guts Frisbee tournament was held in nearby Eagle Harbor.

The Calumet Colosseum has hosted hockey games for more than a century. Photos courtesy of Calumet Colosseum.

When the Calumet National Guard Armory burned down in 1942 and the state bought the arena for use as the Calumet Armory, the local hockey association leased the ice each season. In 2005 the township and the association took over operation and restored the Calumet Colosseum name. For more than a century, the Colosseum has been a center of community activity for hockey, figure skating, open skating, and other events. The lobby walls are lined with historic photos, hockey equipment, skates, and memorabilia.

23 ROCK STAR

What UP natural resource is internationally recognized for its significance?

Jacobsville Sandstone, the unique and beautiful red rock found in the southeast Keweenaw Peninsula, is recognized as a Global Heritage Stone Resource by the International Union of Geological Sciences and UNESCO's International Geoscience Programme. It is one of the first fifteen materials so cited in the world and the only one in the United States to have received the newly established designation. The ancient, high-quality sandstone is a distinctive red, streaked or spotted with white, pink, or brown markings.

Many sandstone quarries were active in the UP from about 1870 to 1915, but the Jacobsville stone was quarried at three main locations between 1880 and 1910. The sandstone was a popular building material for its strength, durability, and aesthetics. It was used extensively in Upper Michigan, Wisconsin, and Minnesota, but it was also shipped to projects in Chicago, St. Louis, Cincinnati, Cleveland, and the East Coast, most notably to build the first Waldorf-Astoria Hotel in New York City.

Examples of sandstone structures in the UP abound, from magnificent churches to homes and mining, municipal, and other buildings, including the Marquette County Courthouse and the Calumet Theatre.

The cliff walls of Jacobsville Sandstone lining Lake Superior between Jacobsville and Rabbit Bay are best seen by kayak, although it's possible to inspect them by wading in the chilly water when the lake is calm.

Sandstone is found in numerous buildings across the UP.

JACOBSVILLE SANDSTONE

WHAT St. Peter Cathedral is a stunning example of a structure made of Jacobsville Sandstone.

WHERE 311 W. Baraga Ave., Marquette

COST Free

PRO TIP Visit on your own or call 906-226-6548 to arrange a guided tour of the cathedral.

24 FLAKES BY THE FOOT

Where can you see how the annual snowfall in the Keweenaw Peninsula measures up?

Snowfall in the Keweenaw Peninsula is legendary, typically starting in October and lasting until May. Snowbanks can take weeks longer to disappear—not surprising when the accumulated heaps of lake-effect snow average five feet but can reach twelve feet tall. An annual snowfall that is measured in hundreds of inches can be tough to visualize, but there's a roadside attraction to assist with that. What looks like a towering thermometer at the side of the highway near the village of Mohawk measures the cumulative amount of white stuff that falls throughout the season. Right there at the top, at 390.4 inches, the snow stick marks the record dump of the winter of 1978–79. That's right, thirty-two and a half feet.

The Keweenaw County Road Commission maintains the snow depth indicator, and its data shows that, indeed, snowfall fluctuates. Years ago, when the thermometer reported the level for the period of 1910 to 1992, the all-time low snowfall was 81.3 inches, in 1930–31. The eighty-two-year average for that era was 187 inches. The gauge now reflects the years 1957 through 2011 and shows a decided increase in snowfall: the low was 161.1 inches in 1999–2000, and the fifty-four-year average was 240.8 inches.

KEWEENAW SNOW STICK

WHAT Roadside thermometer indicates the Keweenaw Peninsula's cumulative snowfall for the year

WHERE US 41/M-26, north of Mohawk

COST Free

PRO TIP Don't plan a winter picnic at the pleasant little Snow Gauge roadside park at the site; it closes for the snowy season.

The snow gauge currently tops out at 390.4 inches, the record snowfall of 1978–79; the arrow indicates the most recent year's total.

Surrounded by Lake Superior, the Keweenaw Peninsula gets a tremendous amount of lake-effect snow, making it the snowiest place east of the Rockies.

25 INDIAN GIVER

Why is there a giant likeness of a Chippewa Indian by the lake in Wakefield?

When he was a lad, Peter Wolf Toth and his family fled their native Hungary and ended up in Ohio. There, he became interested in Native American culture and saw parallels to the injustices that the people of his homeland had experienced. Largely a self-taught artist, Toth carved his first Indian sculpture of stone in La Jolla, California, in 1972. That project inspired his *Trail of the Whispering Giants*, his quest to carve at least one likeness of a Native American in each of the fifty states.

Toth hand-carved his fifty-ninth sculpture in 1988 in Wakefield, alongside Sunday Lake. *Nee-Gaw-Nee-Gaw-Bow ("Leading Man")*, who represents the Chippewa of the area, stands twenty feet tall and was made from a pine tree donated by the Ottawa National Forest. From

NEE-GAW-NEE-GAW-BOW

WHAT Number fifty-nine of seventy-three statues carved of wood by Peter Wolf Toth to honor native people in the United States and Canada. His sculpture of Hungarian King Stephen stands along the Danube River.

WHERE 673 M-28, Wakefield

COST Free

PRO TIP Relax on the deck and admire the adjoining Veterans Memorial alongside beautiful Sunday Lake.

Several of Toth's statues on the *Trail of Whispering Giants* have been destroyed by termites, lightning, and the rare vandal. Michigan lost one of its two sculptures to wood rot; only *Nee-Gaw-Nee-Gaw-Bow* still stands.

Nee-Gaw-Nee-Gaw-Bow *stands twenty feet tall and was carved from a single pine tree donated by the Ottawa National Forest.*

1972 to 1988, Toth traveled the United States and Canada and asked for no payment for his creations; he did receive assistance with food and lodging and the donation of the trees for his works. Toth has said that he studied each log until he visualized the Indian within, and, with mallet and chisel, intertwined the spirit of the tree with the spirit of the Indian.

He calls himself "Indian Giver" not because of the distorted and selfish modern interpretation of the description, but because of the original intent of the native people who, when given a gift, reciprocated with a gift out of respect. Toth's gifts are the sculptures, and in return he asks for a gift of honor and understanding of Native Americans.

26 KETCHUP VS. GRAVY

What's a sure way to start a heated debate in the UP?

The copper and iron mines that brought Cornish immigrants to the UP have been closed for decades, but the hearty meal that the laborers from Cornwall introduced to fellow miners lives on as what could be called the unofficial official comfort food of the region. The pasty (while tasty, it rhymes with nasty) is a simple pie consisting of a meat and root vegetable filling wrapped in a flaky but substantial crust, baked to golden perfection. The pasty could be stashed in a miner's jacket pocket, warmed on a shovel over a candle, and eaten by hand. It was practical sustenance for the men who disappeared into the earth for long, grueling days in the mines. The meal was adopted by other ethnic groups, especially the Finns. Since they outnumbered the Cornish workers, the pasty became identified as a Finnish food.

Pasties are sold in just about every corner of the UP, at roadside stands, restaurants, bars, bakeries, and the freezers of grocery stores. Most Yoopers are loyal to their favorite outlet and are particular about the content of their pies, so it's risky to describe any recipe as "traditional." However, the basic pasty consists of a dough made with lard and a filling of beef, potatoes, onions, rutabaga, and/or carrots, simply seasoned with salt, pepper, and a pat of butter. The dough is folded over and crimped to hold everything together. The real controversy comes next: whether to devour it with ketchup or gravy.

PASTIES

WHAT All-in-one meal, traditionally consisting of a meat and root vegetable mixture in a flaky crust

WHERE Roadside stands, restaurants, and grocery freezers across the UP

COST Usually $5 to $7

PRO TIP The annual Pasty Fest in Calumet features a pasty bake-off, pasty-eating competition, and parade.

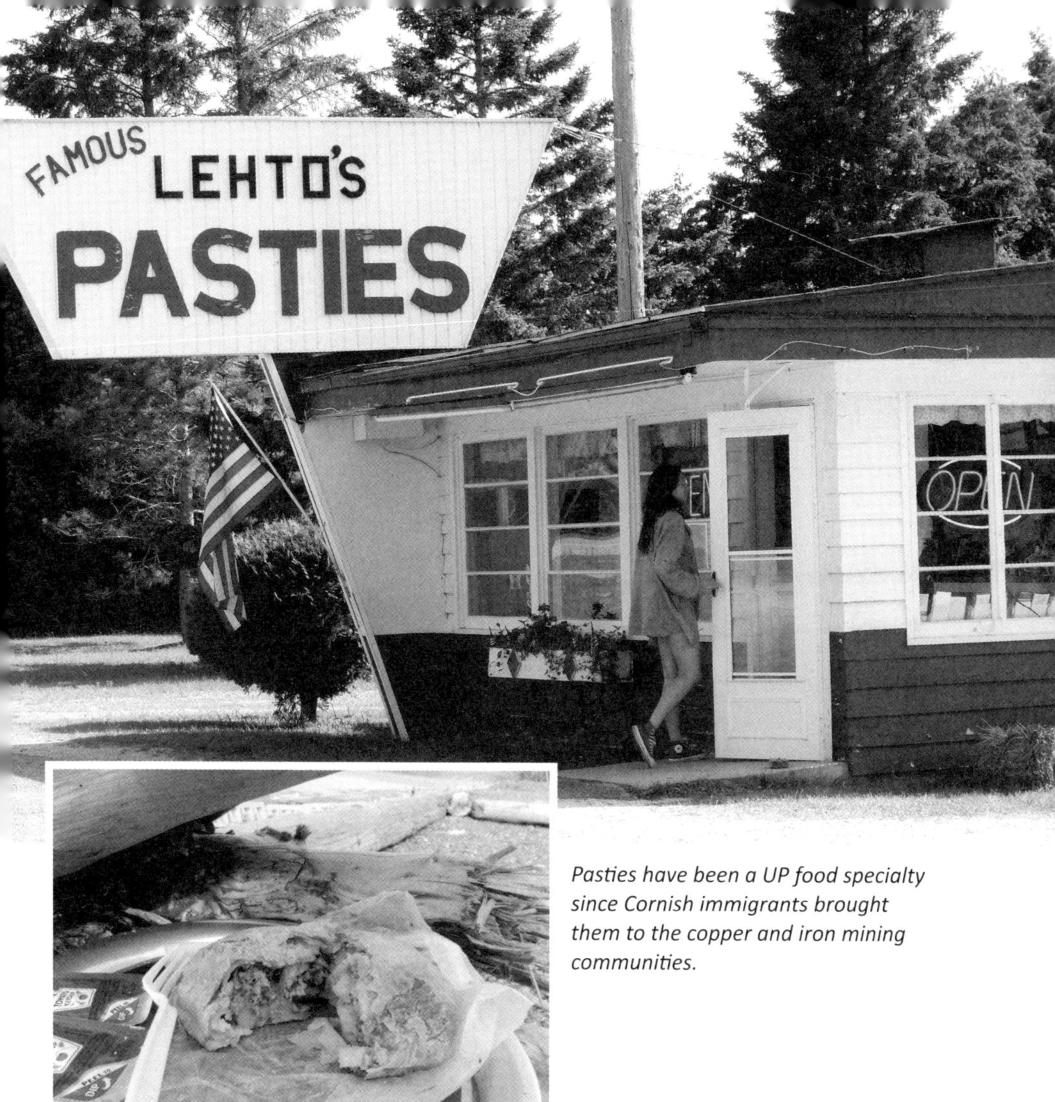

Pasties have been a UP food specialty since Cornish immigrants brought them to the copper and iron mining communities.

Pasties now come in chicken, vegetarian, breakfast, and dessert varieties, and some people have escalated the condiment debate by throwing salsa and sriracha into the ring.

27 PLANE REMARKABLE

Why is the UP one of the few places on earth that you can you see a rare, authentically restored stealth aircraft from WWII?

In 1920 Henry Ford chose a location near Iron Mountain for the production of wooden parts for his automobiles, which required construction of a sawmill, manufacturing plants, and a dam and hydroelectric power plant. By 1923, the area he'd developed was chartered as the village of Kingsford, named for local businessman and Ford dealer Edward G. Kingsford, the husband of Henry's dear cousin Minnie.

During WWII, Ford converted the Kingsford facility to the production of the Waco CG-4A military glider, the most widely used transport for American troops and cargo. These forty-eight-foot-long aircraft, with a wingspan of just over eighty-three feet, were made of painted canvas stretched over a wood and steel tubing frame, with a honeycombed plywood floor. In addition to the pilot and copilot, the Waco CG-4A could carry thirteen troops and their gear, but no parachutes for the "glider riders"—that weight was better allocated to equipment. With no engine or propellers, the gliders were towed behind bombers and released, silently and under darkness, to deliver weapons and troops behind enemy lines. They were the stealth aircraft of their day.

From 1942 to 1945, 13,900 of these gliders were built—4,190 of them at Kingsford. During peak production, 4,500 employees working three around-the-clock shifts assembled eight gliders every twenty-four hours (no small feat considering each one

---

Because Ford had the infrastructure in place, the Kingsford facility was able to produce more gliders at a significantly better price than any other U.S. glider plant.

Volunteers restored one of the gliders built at the plant in Kingsford and created the military museum to showcase it, along with uniforms, artifacts, and other military displays from the Civil War through the wars in Iraq and Afghanistan. Photos courtesy of Iron Mountain Area Tourism.

contained seventy thousand parts). One of those Kingsford gliders was brought back to life, sparked by the donation of a locally built fuselage frame. Over the course of six years, dozens of volunteers dedicated thousands of hours to restoration of the aircraft and construction of a museum to house it. Leading the way was Clyde Unger, whose contribution of fifteen thousand man hours and deep enthusiasm, craftsmanship, and dedication are recognized with a plaque at the museum.

WWII GLIDER AND MILITARY MUSEUM

WHAT Home to a Waco CG-4A Glider, one of only seven of the authentically restored WWII workhorse aircraft in the world

WHERE 302 Kent St., Iron Mountain

COST $8; seniors, $7; students, $4; children, free

PRO TIP Save on a combination ticket that includes the local history and mining museums, and see the largest steam-driven pumping engine built in the United States.

28 MINE BLOWING

Where can you see a machine that moved workers to their job site almost two miles underground?

By the time the California Gold Rush began in 1848, Michigan's copper boom had been underway for several years. The red metal was plentiful and pure. It was the lifeblood of the Keweenaw Peninsula, which is still known as Copper Country some sixty years after the last mining operations ended. Multiple dimensions of the copper story are told through the Keweenaw National Historical Park and the Keweenaw Heritage Sites, a network of independent museums, tours, and other locations related to the copper industry. For a good start in understanding the workings of the mines and the miners who worked them, head to Quincy No. 2 Shaft, the landmark perched above the city of Hancock. Quincy Mine, named "Old Reliable" because it consistently produced high-quality copper—and dividends for its investors—opened in 1848 and, after phasing out operations for decades, closed in 1945.

The three-part, two-hour guided tour begins with an explanation of the world's largest steam-powered hoist. The Nordberg hoist could haul up to five tons of copper from nearly two miles into the earth. At each end of a shift, it lowered and raised the miners, packed into thirty-man cars, to and from their demanding work. The tour continues with everyone clad in the provided hard hats and jackets for the ride aboard the cog-rail tram, down the hill to the

---

The nonprofit, volunteer-run Quincy Mine Hoist Association owns and operates the mine properties, preserving the site and interpreting for the public the history of copper mining in the region.

QUINCY MINE

WHAT Tours that take you above and below ground of one of the most reliably productive copper mines in the country

WHERE 49750 US 41, Hancock

COST For the full tour, ages 55 and up, $40; 13-54, $40; 6-12, $20

PRO TIP Prowl the grounds to photograph abandoned mine buildings in various stages of ruin.

Quincy Mine tours travel to the seventh of ninety-two levels; the lower eighty-five levels are flooded with water.

adit (horizontal mine entrance). There, a tour wagon rolls into the mine for nearly a half mile past old equipment and mining cars, at a depth of seven levels below the earth's surface. Guides talk about the drills used by the miners and their backbreaking and dangerous jobs in the damp and dark environment. Back aboveground, a hoist building and shaft house display artifacts, exhibits, and video and photographic proof of the hard lives lived in the quest for copper.

29 FROM SLOVENIAN HIGH SOCIETY TO SNOWSHOE PRIEST

Why is there a giant statue of a priest holding snowshoes overlooking Lake Superior?

Frederic Baraga was born to a Slovenian family of means in 1797. After studying law, the young man felt called to enter the seminary, and in 1823 he was ordained a priest. Fascinated by missionary work in America, Father Baraga headed across the Atlantic in 1830, and for years, he carried out his missionary work among Native Americans in Michigan's northern Lower Peninsula. He made a dedicated effort to learn the Ottawa language, and in 1832 he printed his first Indian Prayer Book. In 1843 he moved to the UP and the Ojibway band at L'Anse.

There, in the land of long, snowy winters, Father Baraga traveled tremendous distances on snowshoes—often hundreds of miles—to reach far-flung immigrant miners and Native Americans, who affectionately called him the Snowshoe Priest. He was elevated to the first bishop of the diocese of Marquette in 1853 and continued his work until his death in 1868. His remains are interred in a crypt at Marquette's St. Peter Cathedral. Since the 1950s, Venerable Baraga has been under consideration by the Vatican for sainthood.

In addition to the village and county named Baraga, historic Baraga sites across the UP include the Baraga House in Sault Ste. Marie and Indian Lake Mission Chapel near Manistique.

The nonprofit Bishop Baraga Foundation is responsible for the care of the shrine, which was designed by UP sculptor Jack Anderson and dedicated in 1973.

BISHOP BARAGA SHRINE

WHAT Massive sculpture commemorating the Snowshoe Priest of northern Michigan

WHERE 17570 US 41, L'Anse

COST Free; donations accepted

PRO TIP The shrine is open around the clock and is dramatically lit at night.

Bishop Baraga's legacy is depicted in a towering sculpture on a bluff overlooking Keweenaw Bay near Assinins. The thirty-five-foot bronze likeness of the Snowshoe Priest clutches a seven-foot cross in his right hand and a twenty-six-foot-long pair of snowshoes in his left. He floats on a silver cloud supported by five twenty-five-foot-tall beams emanating from tepees that represent five of his missions.

30 ROCK ON

Where will you find the Guinness World Record mass of copper?

"We have the world's finest crystalized copper, plain and simple," says executive director and interim curator Dr. Theodore J. Bornhorst by way of introducing the collection at the A. E. Seaman Mineral Museum at Michigan Tech University. A large sheet of White Pine copper welcomes visitors to the Michigan copper gallery, where examples of the red metal glow. Outside, a pavilion shelters the Guinness World Record-holding seventeen-ton slab of native copper, recovered from the bottom of Lake Superior in 2001. But it's not all about copper. The museum started as the mining school's teaching collection in 1885 and grew into a mineral museum in 1902. Named for its first curator, Arthur Edmund Seaman, it now houses two mineral collections: Michigan Tech's collection of about twenty-five thousand specimens and the University of Michigan's fifteen thousand specimens, including some dating to the late 1700s. It is the definitive assemblage of minerals from Michigan and the Great Lakes region, and it holds some of the best examples of select specimens from around the world. "This is our mineral heritage, our heritage of the planet," says Bornhorst.

It's no accident that the approximately four thousand pieces on public display are artfully arranged and dramatically lit.

A. E. SEAMAN MINERAL MUSEUM

WHAT The official Mineral Museum of Michigan

WHERE 1404 E. Sharon Ave., Houghton

COST Adults, $8; seniors, $7; students with college ID, $4; younger students, $3

PRO TIP Be prepared to be tempted by jewelry and decorative items in the attractive museum shop.

Left: The museum can display only a portion of the collections of Michigan Tech and the University of Michigan.

Top right: The A. E. Seaman Mineral Museum boasts a rock garden, of course. Photo courtesy of A. E. Seaman Mineral Museum.

Above right: The seventeen-ton piece of copper was retrieved from the floor of Lake Superior in 2001. Photo courtesy of A. E. Seaman Mineral Museum.

"We introduce you to their beauty right at the entrance. I want to get you hooked, because minerals are beautiful. The artistic qualities that make a mineral beautiful are no different than what makes art beautiful," Bornhorst explains. Deep and contrasting hues induce oohs and ahhs in the *Beauty of Minerals* exhibit. UV lighting reveals shockingly brilliant colors of specimens in the fluorescent gallery. A stunning, tall purple amethyst cathedral pair is a centerpiece of the popular gemstone display. Once you're captivated, Bornhorst says, "We would like you to learn about why minerals are important to you as a human being."

Fittingly, when construction of the new museum began in 2010, the crew discovered that it sat on two shafts of the Mabbs Vein, a copper mining operation started in 1864 by brothers John and Austin Mabbs.

31 RUSTIC RETREAT

Where can you saw logs in a cabin built of locally sawn logs?

The difficult days of the early 1930s were nowhere more severe than in Keweenaw County, which had bragging rights to the highest unemployment rate in the nation, at 75.2 percent. Members of the local road commission proposed a plan to develop Brockway Mountain Drive and the Keweenaw Park and Golf Course project a mile south of Copper Harbor. Utilizing federal funds available through the Civil Works Administration (and later the Works Progress Administration) on 167 acres of forested land donated by the Keweenaw Copper Company, work began in 1933 with the clearing of trees to carve out the nine-hole golf course.

Harvested logs were used in building the Keweenaw Mountain Lodge and two dozen guest cabins. The main lodge houses the lounge and restaurant in a high-ceilinged room under heavy log rafters, anchored by a massive stone fireplace. The cozy log cabins have wood or gas fireplaces and one, two, or three bedrooms.

KEWEENAW MOUNTAIN LODGE

WHAT Historic resort carved out of the wilderness in the 1930s

WHERE 14252 US 41, Copper Harbor

COST Rates vary for the assortment of one-, two-, and three-bedroom log cabins, from $160 to $325 per night. Moderate meal prices.

PRO TIP The lodge is open through fall color season, a spectacular time to drive the eighteen-mile Scenic Heritage Route along US 41 through a tunnel of trees to Copper Harbor.

Trees cleared to create the nine-hole golf course were used to construct the log main lodge and cozy cabins in the 1930s.

Over the years, a conference center was added. Activities include mountain biking, cross-country and hiking trails, disc golf, and the nine-hole golf course.

Built and operated by the county for more than eighty-five years, the Keweenaw Mountain Lodge is now under private ownership.

32 CURE FOR THE COMMON SIGN

Which UP county has the swingingest road signage in Michigan?

In the northernmost part of the UP, the air is clear, the water is cold, the pace is slow, people are few, and the road signs are retro rustic cool. Handcrafted of dark brown, heavy timbers and scalloped wood placards, the signs are lettered in a deep orange and white; some include a colorful map for orientation. They reinforce what so many visitors observe about Keweenaw County: traveling through this area is like stepping back in time.

That impression comes through deliberate effort on the part of the Keweenaw County Planning Commission. As stated in its Blueprint for Tomorrow 2017, "Keweenaw County has rustic signage as a binding feature . . . The signs identify roads, rivers, scenic, and historic sites among other characteristics in the County. Maintained by

KEWEENAW'S RUSTIC ROAD SIGNAGE

WHAT Retro, handcrafted road signage

WHERE Throughout Keweenaw County

COST Free

PRO TIP If you like the sign paint color, ask for Keweenaw County Brown from Sherwin Williams.

The original signs of this design date to the 1930s and were made by workers in federal jobs programs. Replacements and new signs continue that style.

The rustic signage has been a Keweenaw County characteristic since the 1930s.

the County Road Commission, this feature provides a local flair to otherwise common signage."

Of the directional and interpretive signs posted throughout the county, the one closest to the tip of the peninsula is positioned beyond the village of Copper Harbor and marks the start of US Highway 41. The description and map illustrate the 1,990-mile link between the Lake Superior shore and the Atlantic Ocean. It also recognizes the late Byron Muljo, who designed and built many signs for the Keweenaw County Road Commission, including those at the Snow Gauge and Brockway Mountain Drive—and his own tribute.

33 SKETE SWEETS AND SCOOFIES

What are monks doing along the Keweenaw's Lake Superior shore?

Unless you're prepared for the sight, the glistening golden domes that appear out of the Keweenaw forest near Jacob's Falls can be a bit jarring. But if you're looking for the Jampot, you know you're at the right place; the bakery is across the road. The domes top Holy Transfiguration Skete, a Byzantine Catholic monastery that was built, by jar of jam and jelly, by the monks of the Jampot. It started in 1983, when the two founders followed their vocation and moved to this wilderness with no idea of how they would survive. They bought some rundown cabins and an old hamburger joint, barely made it through their first winter, and, as monks do, prayed a lot. Inspired by the bounty of wild blueberries, raspberries, strawberries, and thimbleberries all around them, they learned to turn foraged fruits into the Poorrock Abbey preserves that they sell, along with caramels, truffles, and fresh-from-the-oven muffins and cookies, at their snug shop.

Over their decades they have built the monastery and their business through a steady stream of repeat and new customers, and online year-round. Visitors are welcome to stroll the monastic gardens and follow the footpath they are carving out of their wooded property. The sometimes-steep trail winds past creeks, rocks, wildflowers, and wildlife. Be on

---

In an online invitation to enjoy their grounds, the monks observe, "In our often all too busy modern, fast-paced lives, gardens are more necessary to our spiritual well-being than perhaps ever before."

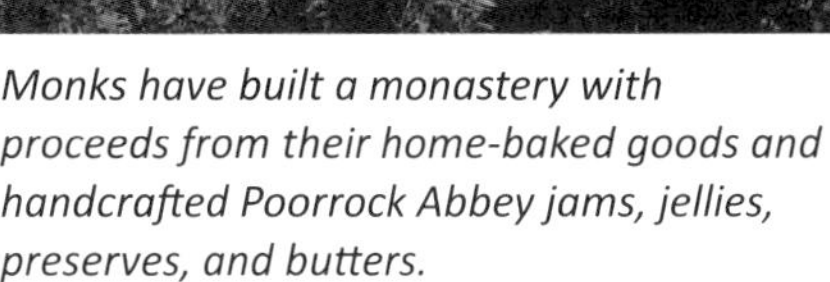
Monks have built a monastery with proceeds from their home-baked goods and handcrafted Poorrock Abbey jams, jellies, preserves, and butters.

the lookout for the tiny people reputed to live in the gorge of Jacob's Creek. The good-humored monks have named them Scoofies, and in an illustrated online book they imagine, "If ever there was a place that seemed suited to habitation by elves, faeries, gnomes, or leprechauns, our gorge was it. Its many nooks, cracks, and crannies would provide perfect shelter for such little people—should they happen to exist."

JAMPOT

WHAT Jams, preserves, baked goods, and confections made and sold by monks

WHERE 6559 M-26, Eagle Harbor

COST Nine-ounce jars of preserves, etc., $8 and up, depending on kind; bakery items vary

PRO TIP Arrive early in the day for bakery items; when they're out, they're out.

34 STREET TALK

What road in Hancock is named for a cow pasture?

From the late 1800s into the early twentieth century, a wave of Finnish immigrants made their way from Finland to work in the copper mines of the UP. In Hancock, a city where a large percentage of the population is of Finnish descent, some of the street signs bear names in both English and Finnish, such as Quincy/Valta Katu and Ryan/Kukkula Katu. Even in an area where unusual names are common, there's one road sign that may cause a double take—and a chuckle from those in the know. It is Kowsit Lats Road located on Quincy Hill, where many Finnish workers lived near the Quincy Mine Hoist. It wasn't unusual back then for families to have their own cow at their home, and the mining company provided a communal pasture where their livestock could graze.

With that bit of background, to understand the origin of Kowsit Lats you need to imagine the linguistic logistics

KOWSIT LATS

WHAT Description of a cow pasture with roots in the "Finglish" vernacular

WHERE Off US 41 at Quincy Hill, Hancock

COST Free

PRO TIP There's a nice view of Portage Lake and the cities of Hancock and Houghton from this spot.

Wilbur "Wimpy" Salmi, a local character with a dose of dry Finnish humor, created a green and white sign pointing the way to Kowsit Lats. It later received an official street sign and map designation.

Wilbur "Wimpy" Salmi created the square sign in the foreground in the 1980s; now only the official street sign in the background remains. Photo by Kathryn Remlinger.

required of people whose first language is Finnish when those people are speaking English. In the Finnish language, the letter *C* doesn't exist; *K* covers that sound. There is no *SH* sound in Finnish, so *S* was substituted. Since the combination *FL* is absent from the Finnish language, it was replaced with just the *L*. This mash-up of sounds and pronunciations became known as "Finglish." So, the area where cows grazed and did their business—known as "Cows*it Flats" in English—was pronounced, in Finglish, "Kowsit Lats."

35 THE FUNGUS AMONG US

Where can you take a bite out of a one-hundred-square-foot mushroom pizza?

In 1992, when researchers first reported discovery of a massive *Armillaria gallica* near Crystal Falls in the Western UP, they declared the thirty-seven-acre, 1,500-year-old "humongous fungus" the largest and possibly oldest organism on record. Although it survives underground and out of sight, the fungus sprouts honey mushrooms, which are edible and harvested in late summer to early fall. Michigan's mushroom glory was short-lived, however; soon after the revelation in the UP, a specimen of *Armillaria ostoyea*, covering more than three square miles and perhaps eight thousand years old, was identified in eastern Oregon. Recent testing indicates that Michigan's fungus is actually spread over 185 acres, and it is now estimated to be at least 2,500 years old. Still no match for its western rival, but something to be celebrated nonetheless.

HUMONGOUS FUNGUS FEST

WHAT Annual celebration in August of one of the largest and oldest-known living organisms on earth

WHERE Downtown Crystal Falls

COST Free

PRO TIP Sign up for a mushroom-foraging excursion for guidance on finding edible 'shrooms.

Pointing out that the organism in Oregon is a different species and does not grow contiguously, Crystal Falls refers to its humongous fungus as the "oldest, largest, contiguous life-form on earth."

Left: The celebrated Humongous Fungus honey mushrooms don't show until after the festival in their honor, but you can gather other edibles from the forest floor on a guided 'shroom hunt. Photo courtesy of Iron County Economic Chamber Alliance.

Right: The giant mushroom pizza is a tasty highlight of the annual festival. Photo courtesy of Iron County Economic Chamber Alliance.

Since the discovery of the tourist attraction beneath its forest floor, the Crystal Falls community has honored its hidden asset with the Humongous Fungus Festival in August. Highlights of the three-day event include a guided mushroom-hunting excursion, a mushroom cook-off and cooking demonstrations, a ten-foot-square mushroom pizza, and the Fungus Fest Parade.

36 TRANQUIL CAMPGROUND

Where can you sleep under the stars next to a Native American burial ground?

On the south shore of Chicaugon Lake, the Anishinaabe, or Ojibwa, established a settlement that lasted until 1891. At that time, Meshkawaanagonebi, known as Chief John Edwards, moved his people further west to distance themselves from the iron mining boom. In 1924 Iron County purchased the property for use as a public park, which is named in honor of Chief Edward's wife, Biindigeyaasinokwe. Her name was shortened to Biindige and interpreted as Pentoga.

Pentoga Park is a beautiful spot for picnics, swimming, boating, fishing, hiking the two and a half miles on the Brule River Trail, and camping. Its 135-site campground is adjacent to the Native American burial grounds, which date to the time when this was the Ojibwa village. The preserved cemetery has traditional Indian spirit houses marking the graves. Spirit houses, sometimes referred to as grave houses or grave shelters, are small, sacred structures that provide shelter to the souls of the departed. They are a place for loved ones to place food, arrows, beads, and items needed to travel to the spirit world. It's not the only such burial ground in the UP, but it's the only one next to a campground.

The Pinery Indian Cemetery near L'Anse has been used by the Zeba Indian Mission United Methodist Church since 1840 and has both stone markers and traditional Native American spirit houses.

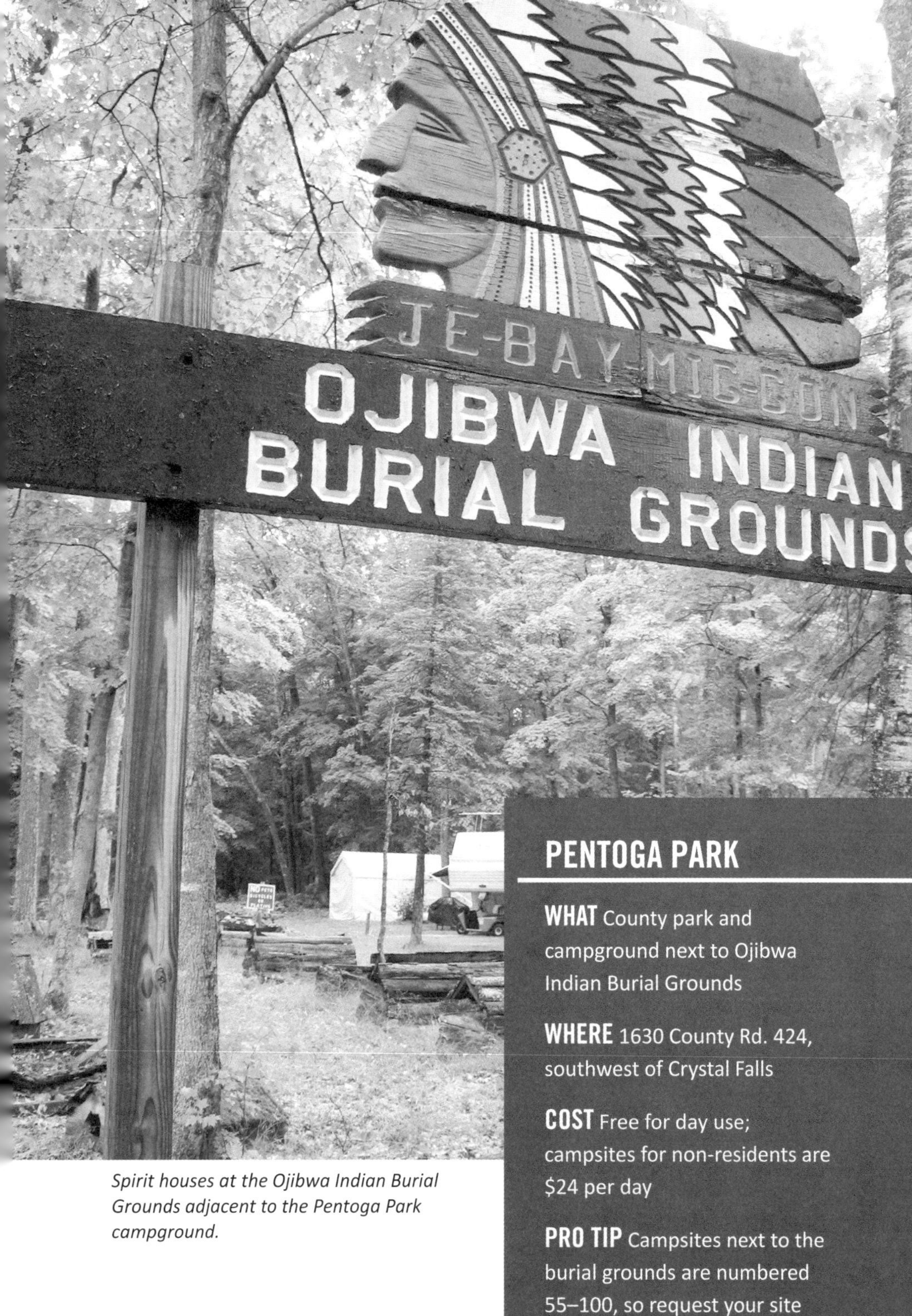

Spirit houses at the Ojibwa Indian Burial Grounds adjacent to the Pentoga Park campground.

PENTOGA PARK

WHAT County park and campground next to Ojibwa Indian Burial Grounds

WHERE 1630 County Rd. 424, southwest of Crystal Falls

COST Free for day use; campsites for non-residents are $24 per day

PRO TIP Campsites next to the burial grounds are numbered 55–100, so request your site accordingly.

37 CALL OF THE WILD

Where is the best place in the world to learn about moose and wolves?

Remote and rugged, the largest island in Lake Superior is a place of wild beauty, accessible only by boat or seaplane from mid-April through October. Isle Royale National Park is an archipelago of more than four hundred small islands surrounding the forty-five-mile-long-by-nine-mile-wide main island. There are no roads on Isle Royale; getting around is by foot on 165 miles of trails, paddling, or boating from point to point by water taxi or on scheduled excursions. Sleeping is at one of three dozen campgrounds or the Rock Harbor Lodge. Not surprisingly, given the challenges in reaching and exploring Isle Royale, it is one of the least-visited national parks in the United States, with only about eighteen thousand visitors annually.

This is the setting for the Wolf–Moose Project, the longest-running predator–prey study on the planet. Moose first made their way to the island in the early 1900s, and in the winter of 1948 a pack of wolves crossed an ice bridge from Canada. In 1958 Durward Allen, a professor of wildlife ecology at Purdue University, initiated the study of the dynamics

ISLE ROYALE NATIONAL PARK

WHAT A four-hundred-island archipelago that was made a national park in 1940

WHERE 55 miles off the UP's Keweenaw Peninsula, 15 miles from Minnesota in northwest Lake Superior

COST Depends on mode of transportation to the island (ferry or seaplane), activities and excursions at the park, and whether you are camping or staying at the Rock Harbor Lodge

PRO TIP Book early; although still one of the least-visited national parks, Isle Royale is growing in popularity as a destination, and accommodations are limited.

Moose usually give birth in May to calves that weigh between twenty and thirty pounds. By fall, the young moose weigh three hundred pounds. Photo courtesy of Wolves & Moose of Isle Royale.

of these animals. In the 1970s Rolf Peterson, a Michigan Tech professor of wildlife ecology, took over the project. With his wife, Candy, and additional researchers, Peterson continues to observe wolf–moose behaviors, interaction, genetics, health, death, and their fluctuating populations. In 2018 just two wolves remained on the island, allowing the number of moose to balloon to a near record 2,060. The vegetation isn't sufficient to support that number, and the controversial decision was made to relocate wolves to the park in an attempt to restore the balance lost between predator and prey. Each summer, committed (and very fit) volunteers backpack into the wilderness on guided, week-long Moosewatch Expeditions to search for moose bones for the study.

> "To understand nature it also helps to observe an ecosystem where human impact is limited. . . . Isle Royale is remarkable, because nature runs wild there." —Website, Wolves & Moose of Isle Royale

38 DIG THIS

Where can you rappel into the depths of a copper mine and learn to operate mining equipment?

It wasn't something he aspired to, the way kids say they want to grow up to be a firefighter or a social media influencer. But after earning a degree in mining engineering at Michigan Tech University in Houghton, Matt Portfleet decided to buy an old copper mine and operate it as a tourist attraction.

His Adventure Mining Company in Greenland offers a taste of what it was like for miners to descend into the earth to extract the red metal in the country's first mineral rush, which began in the early 1840s—years ahead of the better-known Gold Rush out west. By the late 1800s Michigan was supplying more than 75 percent of the nation's copper, but the industry slowed in the early 1900s and the era came to a close in the 1960s.

ADVENTURE MINE TOURS

WHAT See what it was like to be a miner in Michigan's Copper Country.

WHERE 200 Adventure Ave., Greenland

COST Adult tours range from $16 to $120

PRO TIP Wear a jacket; the temperature in the mine is a steady forty-eight degrees. Sturdy, closed-toe footwear is required.

Guided Adventure Mine tours offer varying degrees of difficulty and range from walk-throughs suitable for families to

---

The Miner's Revenge Mountain Bike Race in mid-July travels the area's rugged, forested terrain and even goes underground, into the mine, for a portion of the course.

When the only light comes from the headlamp on your helmet, you appreciate the dark and dangerous world of the miner. Interior photos courtesy of Adventure Mine Tours.

the challenging Miner's Tour that requires crawling through tight sections and rappelling eighty feet into darkness. The five-to-six-hour Captain's Tour ventures deep into the mine's lower levels and is fueled by a pasty lunch, the miner's meat-and-vegetable meal in a crust. For the authentic miner experience, the only light comes from the provided headlamps, the ground is uneven, the air dank, and resident bat sightings almost guaranteed.

Those who want to dig further into the hard work of mining can take a six-hour underground workshop, with hands-on learning and utilizing tools from air compressors to pneumatic rock drills.

39 IT WAS A BLAST

What was NASA doing at the tip of the Keweenaw Peninsula?

At the end of a long and bumpy trail, on the Lake Superior shore, a small marker and remnants of a launch pad indicate the history of the spot known as the Keweenaw Rocket Range, which functioned from 1964 to 1971. The University of Michigan proposed the project to NASA as one of several such sites across the country built for the purpose of collecting meteorological data.

The small- and medium-range rockets launched at the Keweenaw location were instrument-carrying sounding rockets. The first, a six-foot Arcas, lifted off on August 6, 1964, to an altitude of forty-one miles; five additional Arcas launches took place through September. The site was used to run tests for the WEBROC and NOMAD projects, which would place buoys in distant ocean locations to remotely launch small Mighty Mouse rockets to gather weather information.

KEWEENAW ROCKET RANGE

WHAT Site of rocket launches from 1964 to 1971

WHERE Rocket Range Tr., at the tip of the Keweenaw Peninsula

COST Free

PRO TIP The route to the site begins where US 41 ends. It is a rough, four-to-five-mile trail, and it may be better to hike or ride a mountain bike to the location. Even experienced riders end up pushing their bikes quite a bit due to the challenging trail.

In 1970, NASA wanted to launch two Nike-Apaches, which measured more than twenty-eight feet tall and were capable of traveling to more than one hundred miles above the earth. Testing of the larger rockets was restricted to the winter months to avoid passing freighter traffic. The team

Little remains of the equipment, but a marker commemorates Keweenaw's contribution to NASA's efforts. Photo courtesy of Exploring Off the Beaten Path.

also had to be concerned about the winds affecting the trajectory toward Marquette, to the southeast, and with rockets crossing the international border with Canada, which cuts through the middle of Lake Superior. Blizzard conditions delayed the launches, which finally took place, successfully, on January 29 and 31 of 1971. A witness to the January 29 launch recalls, "The rocket peaked out at 118 miles high over Lake Superior. What a blast! The heat melted the three-foot-deep snow to within one hundred feet of me."

The temporary structures put in place for the project were dismantled, and finally, in the year 2000, a marker was installed to commemorate the work done at the secluded site.

The marker reads: "The State of Michigan established a rocket range on this site which was used from 1964–1971. Michigan's first rocket to enter space was launched from this site on Jan. 29, 1971. In tribute to the historic work done in the field of rocketry, this memorial stone was placed in the summer of the year 2000 by NASA."

40 USS SELFIE

Where can you take your picture on an unsinkable boat built of rocks?

Cruising along US 41 north of Calumet, you can't miss the stone boat permanently docked at the side of the highway in Kearsarge. The old mining community was named after the USS *Kearsarge* by a Calumet and Hecla mine company employee who'd come to the UP after serving aboard the Civil War sloop. The stone boat is sometimes called the USS *Kearsarge*, but it bears no resemblance to that naval ship. It's a figment of the imagination of idled miners who were employed by the Civil Works Administration (predecessor to the Works Progress Administration) to build the Keweenaw Mountain Resort and Brockway Mountain Drive, as well as three of these boats.

They built the roadside attraction of sandstone, poorrock, and concrete and equipped it with odd pipes for stacks and portholes and a rock drill for the machine gun. The veterans' memorial and flagpoles are recent additions. Of the three boats, the *Kearsarge* is the most accessible and selfie-worthy. A second sits in Centennial Heights and the third has crumbled to rubble.

Raise a glass to the veterans and USS *Kearsarge* with Stone Ship Stout, an oatmeal stout from Brickside Brewery in Copper Harbor. It's on tap at the brew pub and sold by the bottle in limited amounts in the Keweenaw; look for the Stone Boat on the label.

USS *KEARSARGE*

WHAT A stone boat built in 1933–34, and a more recently added monument to area veterans

WHERE US 41, Kearsarge

COST Free

PRO TIP Go ahead and climb on the boat, as generations of kids have done.

Idled miners working on federally funded projects in the Keweenaw in the 1930s built three stone boats of scrap materials.

The sloop USS *Kearsarge* (1861 to 1894) has had three namesakes: a battleship (1898–1920), an aircraft carrier (1946–1970), and a still active amphibious assault ship commissioned in 1993.

41 YOOPER DEFINED

Who invented the term Yooper?

It was big news across the UP in 2014 when Merriam-Webster decided that Yooper, defined as the term for "a native or resident of the Upper Peninsula of Michigan—used as a nickname," deserved a spot in its dictionary. It cites its etymology as "*yoop*- (from the abbreviation *UP*) + -ER" and the year of the first known use of Yooper as 1975. It just so happens that in 1975, Jim DeCaire and a bunch of musicmaking buddies released their first recording as Da Yoopers, a band that uses coarse comedy and exaggerated regional dialect in original tunes about life in the UP.

The band and its songs and skits about deer camp, shoveling snow, and other aspects of UP life were a hit, and DeCaire opened Da Yoopers Tourist Trap, a souvenir store and roadside attraction on steroids. Its high-visibility spot outside of Ishpeming on the highway stops traffic with displays like Eddy, one of two working wood-burning tractors in the United States, and Big

DA YOOPERS TOURIST TRAP

WHAT Indoor/outdoor roadside attraction and souvenir shop that epitomizes Yooper humor

WHERE 490 N. Steel St. (at US 41/M-28), Ishpeming

COST Free to see, but spending on souvenirs is highly encouraged

PRO TIP Bring your warped sense of humor.

Merriam-Webster won't commit to recognizing the UP term "trolls," for people who live "under" the Mackinac Bridge, stating, "That nickname is still at this point too regional for entry in our dictionaries."

Yooper humor and ingenuity are on full display at Da Yooper Tourist Trap, a roadside attraction and souvenir store.

Ernie, the four-thousand-pound, thirty-five-foot-long working rifle. Big Gus, at twenty-two feet eleven inches, was declared by Guinness in 1996 as the world's largest working chainsaw.

Step inside the Tourist Trap store for your copy of Da Yoopers' "best of" CD with the original hits "Second Week of Deer Camp" and "Rusty Chevrolet." Or pick up a DVD of *Escanaba in da Moonlight*, Michigan actor Jeff Daniels's 2001 movie about a family deer camp. Gifts run the gamut from T-shirts and mugs to a cribbage board shaped like da UP, from sauna soap and nice home decor pieces to a line of Big Foot items (Sasquatch sightings are a UP thing).

42 LIGHTING UP AT THE POINT

Why does the aroma of cigar smoke waft mysteriously through the lighthouse at Seul Choix Point?

With 3,200 miles of Great Lakes shoreline, Michigan has more lighthouses than any other state, and about fifty of the 129 beacons are in the UP. One especially worthwhile lighthouse to visit is at Seul Choix Point, a narrow, rocky Lake Michigan peninsula east of Manistique. The name, pronounced *Sis-shwa*, is French for "only choice" and was given to the site by voyageurs who found it their only hope for refuge in a storm. The temporary first light was lit in 1892, with the permanent structure and lighthouse completed in 1895. The seventy-eight-foot-tall white conical tower is topped with a handsome ten-sided cast-iron lantern room. Automated in 1972, it is one of the few active lights open to visitors. It's ninety-six steps to the top of the lighthouse for views of Lake Michigan, freighter traffic, and, on a clear day, Beaver Island.

The entry fee includes admission to the two-story red-brick antiques-furnished home, lighthouse museum, fog signal building, oil house, boat house, a movie, and the grounds. A museum collection highlight is a dugout canoe, an estimated 150 to 300 years old, that was found in the sand on the point. As a bonus, many visitors and volunteer docents have reported encounters with several ghosts at Seul Choix, especially the cigar-smoking Captain Joseph Willie Townshend. He was

---

In 1988 volunteers formed the Gulliver Historical Society to restore, operate, and care for the lighthouse in cooperation with the Michigan Department of Natural Resources.

Visitors have seen the late lighthouse keeper Townshend peering through the window at Seul Choix Point Light, an active navigational aid that is open to visitors.

lightkeeper from 1901 until he died in an upstairs bedroom in 1910. Stories of the aroma of cigar smoke, tableware rearranged, and furniture moved contribute to Seul Choix's reputation as one of Michigan's most haunted lighthouses.

SEUL CHOIX POINT LIGHTHOUSE

WHAT The seventy-eight-foot-tall tower is at the center of a well-tended museum complex.

WHERE 905 S. Seul Choix Pointe Rd., eight miles south of US 2, Gulliver

COST Adults, $5; youth, $2

PRO TIP Pack a picnic; there are tables for relaxing and the rocky beach to comb for treasures.

43 SUPER YOOPER DOME

Where will you find the world's largest wooden domed stadium?

You don't have to be a sports geek to be a fan of the Superior Dome at Northern Michigan University in Marquette. Looking like an alien spacecraft (for very large ETs) that landed near the Lake Superior shore, it has been a campus and city landmark since it opened in 1991. Designed by TMP Architecture in Bloomfield Hills, Michigan, the multipurpose facility is home to the NMU Wildcats football team as well as basketball, volleyball, soccer, tennis, field hockey, lacrosse, softball, and track and field events. Its mechanically retractable synthetic turf is the largest of its kind in the world.

Measuring 536 feet in diameter, the Yooper Dome, as most people call it, ranks as the fifth-largest domed structure in the world. But the other four are made of steel, so the UP claims the title of world's largest wooden domed stadium. Its geodesic dome is constructed of

SUPERIOR DOME

WHAT The Northern Michigan University sports complex, one of the world's largest domed structures

WHERE 1401 Presque Isle Ave., Marquette

COST Free to see; fee for events

PRO TIP Lace up your walking shoes and join those doing laps on the indoor track on weekdays (except during events).

The Superior Dome is designed to support snow weighing up to sixty pounds per square inch and withstand winds of up to eighty miles per hour.

The igloo-like Superior Dome is often called the Yooper Dome.

The Yooper Dome's interior Douglas fir beams are a thing of beauty. Photo courtesy of TMP Architecture/photo by Gary Quesada, Balthazar Korab, Ltd.

781 Douglas fir beams and 108.5 miles of fir decking, covers 5.1 acres, and reaches 14.1 stories in height. It has permanent seating for eight thousand fans and can accommodate up to sixteen thousand for assemblies.

In 2017, NBC's Al Roker came to the Yooper Dome to coach 634 NMU students to a Guinness World Record for the largest game of freeze tag, but that achievement was crushed the following year by 1,393 players in Belgium. NMU can still brag that it's the home of the world-record game of freeze tag that was played under the world's largest wooden domed stadium.

STUMP PRAIRIE (page 140)

ART WITH A REPURPOSE (page 114)

DIG THIS (page 76)

STORYBOOK COTTAGE (page 192)

FROM SLOVENIAN HIGH SOCIETY TO SNOWSHOE PRIEST (page 58)

SAVED BY THE BELLAIRE (page 112)

IF THEY COULD SEE IT NOW (page 120)

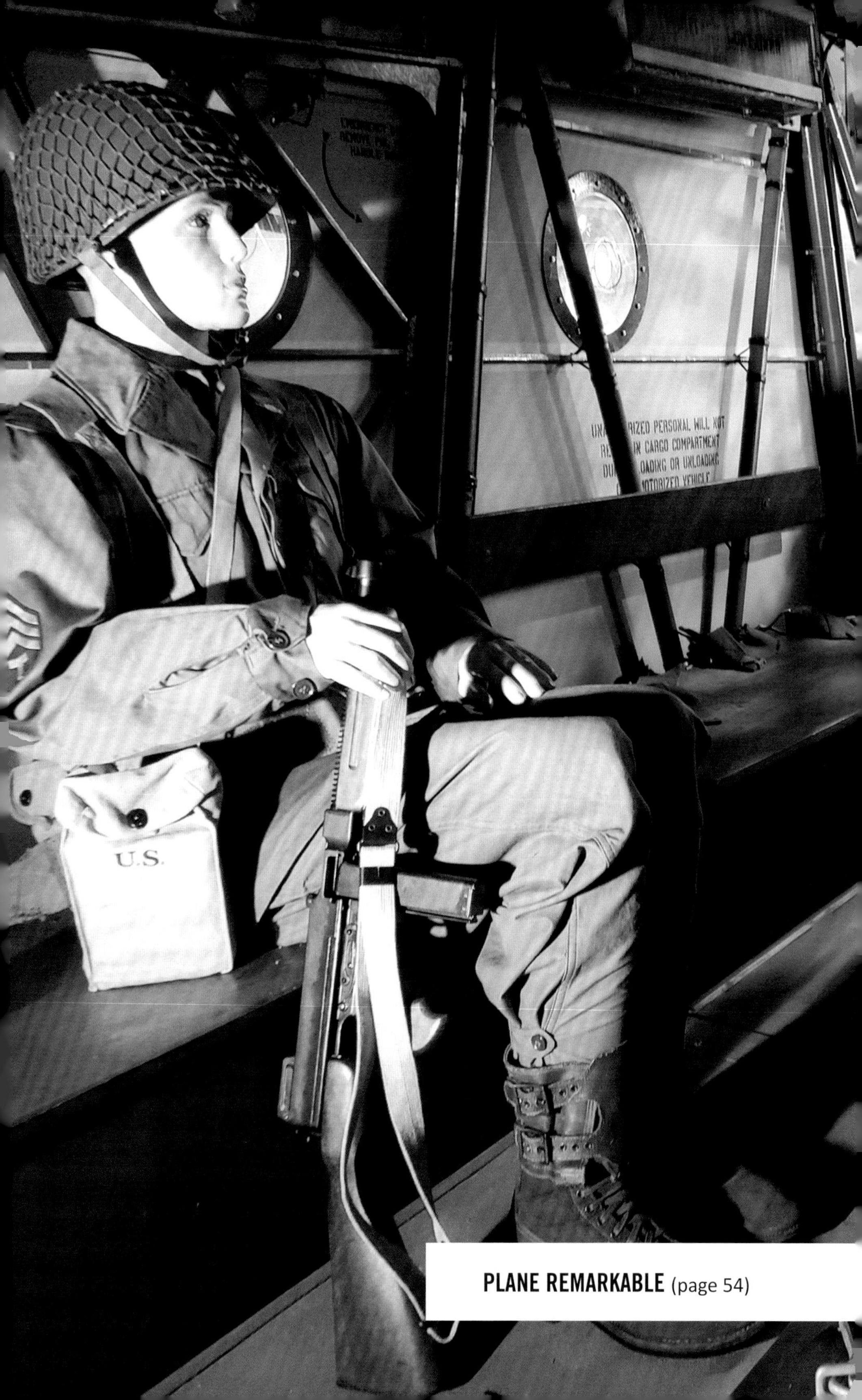

PLANE REMARKABLE (page 54)

KARST QUEST (page 172)

BEST LAID PLANS (page 2)

FUDGE FACTOR (page 146)

FROZEN IN TIME (page 26)

RARE EARTH (page 194)

BEAR NECESSITIES (page 152)

LASTING IMPRESSIONS (page 148)

A BRIDGE TOO FAR (page 142)

44 FAKE NEWS, CIRCA 1913

What happened when a former U.S. president traveled to Marquette to defend himself in a libel suit against a UP newspaper?

The controversy about media truthfulness in politics is nothing new, as Theodore Roosevelt proved in a sensational trial in Marquette. After serving as president upon the assassination of William McKinley, Roosevelt was elected to office in 1904 but lost to William Howard Taft in 1908. Roosevelt's split from the Republican party and his platform as the Progressive "Bull Moose" Party candidate was radical enough to shake up conservative Republican party faithful including George Newett, the unabashedly partisan publisher of the *Iron Ore* newspaper in Ishpeming, a city west of Marquette.

In an editorial, Newett stated that "Roosevelt lies, and curses in a most disgusting way, he gets drunk too, and that not infrequently, and all of his intimates know about it." Roosevelt, whose boisterous persona was

MARQUETTE COUNTY COURTHOUSE

WHAT The Victorian setting for Theodore Roosevelt's suit against a slanderous editorial

WHERE 234 W. Baraga Ave., Marquette

COST Free to see, when court is not in session

PRO TIP The courtroom is usually empty at lunchtime, so that's a good time to step inside the elaborate courtroom with its spectacular glass-domed ceiling.

Roosevelt stated that he'd filed the suit "to deal with these slanders so that never again will it be possible for any man in good faith to repeat them."

NUMBER 245. MARQUETTE, MICHIGAN, TUESDAY AFTERNOON, MAY 27, 1913. PRICE THREE CENTS

OOSEVELT ON THE STAND

ENT IN WITNESS CHAIR SWEARS HE NEVER DRUNK A TAIL OR A HIGHBALL IN HIS LIFE—SAYS HE RARELY S MINT JULEPS—AS FOR BRANDY HE NEVER DRINKS MORE THAN HE DOES WHISKEY—WHEN CAMPAIGN-E DRINKS MILK BEFORE RETIRING.

EXAMINED BY ATTORNEY W. P. BELDEN

STATEMENT OF PROSECUTION

Top left and top right: Theodore Roosevelt testifies on his own behalf in the Roosevelt–Newett libel case in the Marquette County Courthouse. Photo courtesy of Underwood & Underwood Library of Congress *New York World-Telegram* and the *Sun Newspaper* Photograph Collection (Library of Congress).

Right: The Marquette County Courthouse was the scene of Theodore Roosevelt's "Famous Libel Suit" in 1913.

often characterized by political opponents as volatile and drunken behavior, rarely—by many accounts—drank alcohol. He decided to take on Newett in what was called the "Famous Libel Suit." He and an entourage of two dozen notables arrived in Marquette to much fanfare in May of 1913. At the Marquette County Courthouse, stellar character witnesses and Roosevelt's own testimony, as he recounted tales of his presidency, hunting expeditions, and Rough Rider adventures, refuted Newett's accusation—and made great copy for major newspapers and wire services.

After five days, Newett admitted that he'd been wrong. The court's statement declared, "The publisher of a newspaper may freely discuss the fitness of a person for public office, he may lawfully communicate to the public any fact within his knowledge respecting the official acts, character or conduct, so long as he states as facts only the truth." A satisfied Roosevelt requested and received the lowest possible award of six cents and supposedly said, "That's about the price of a GOOD paper." (The *Iron Ore* sold for three cents.)

45 RIP ROVER

Where can you tour the factory of the first pet casket company?

The death of a pet can be as sad an experience as the loss of any other family member or friend. Until the 1960s, not much attention had been paid to giving a proper burial to the dogs, cats, snakes, birds, and other animal members of the household. But Dennis Hoegh (pronounced Hoyg) was thinking about it. At his home in Iowa, he handcrafted prototypes of pet caskets out of fiberglass and tried, without luck, to dig up interest in his peculiar product. Hoegh ended up moving to Michigan to make gun cases for Marble Arms, the Gladstone-based producer of gun sights and outdoor gear.

In 1966 Hoegh launched his pet casket company—the first in the country, and probably the world—in Gladstone. Although the company has changed hands, it continues to produce a variety of sizes, styles, and colors of pet caskets that are vacuum formed of high-impact plastic styrene. Hoegh Industries also creates coordinating pads, pillows, and blankets, as well as cremation urns and memorial markers and plaques designed to remember dearly departed family members that happen to be pets. Tours are available by advance arrangement.

Pet casket pioneer Dennis Hoegh was also a leader in the development of pet cemeteries, the growth of which could only be good for the business he ran with his wife, Jeanne.

Hoegh creates caskets for pets of all sizes, from parakeets to Great Pyrenees. Photo courtesy of Hoegh Pet Casket Company.

HOEGH PET CASKET COMPANY TOUR

WHAT Tour the showroom and factory of the first pet casket company.

WHERE 311 Delta Ave., Gladstone

COST Free

PRO TIP Call 800-236-0416 in advance to set up a tour, offered Monday through Friday.

46 GET TOASTED

Where can you dunk a piece of history in your coffee?

It's dry, crunchy, and isn't visually dazzling. But the twice-baked, cinnamon-coated toast, known as *korppu* in Finnish, has been a staple on the shelves of Yooper pantries since 1928, when Jorma Syrannen started the Trenary Home Bakery at his farm in the tiny mid-UP town of Trenary. The Hallinen family bought the bakery in 1950 and kept the tradition going for more than fifty years. The current owners, Brianna Wynsma and Marco Dossena, are committed to delivering the same Trenary Toast that generations of Yoopers have grown up with, following the same recipe of thickly sliced white bread, baked with the same cinnamon-sugar topping, and then baked again, and packaged sixteen slices to the same, simple, brown bags.

It's an old-fashioned operation, where bakery employees handcraft and package the toast—up to nine hundred bags per day—and bake the other goodies sold in the adjoining café, online, and at a growing list of outlets across the UP and beyond. In addition to the famous toast, favorite bakery items are the cinnamon bread and *limpu*, a Finnish sourdough rye with caraway seeds, that has been a specialty since 1928. In its more than ninety years, the line of Trenary Toast flavors has grown beyond the original cinnamon to include plain, vanilla, cinnamon-raisin, chocolate chip, and cardamom varieties.

TRENARY TOAST

WHAT Traditional Finnish toast handmade by the tray-full since 1928

WHERE E2918 M-67, Trenary

COST Bags of 16 slices retail for about $5

PRO TIP Dunk the toast quickly in a cup of coffee, or break it into chunks and drop it in a bowl of milk to soften it and bring out the flavor.

Trenary Toast is a hands-on operation; even the name on each bag is stamped by hand. Photo by TJ Kozak.

While dunking the toast in a strong cup of coffee is still a time-honored ritual, now it's possible to nibble on Trenary Toast dipped in a choice of milk or dark chocolate while sipping an espresso.

47 SAVED BY THE BELLAIRE

How was one of the UP's natural wonders rescued from its use as a trash dump?

There's a reason the Native Americans called it the "Mirror of Heaven." The still and crystal water of Michigan's largest spring reflects the sky, clouds, and surrounding woods while eerily magnifying the fallen, submerged trees. Kitch-iti-kipi (just say "Big Spring") measures two hundred feet across, and its waters bubble at a rate of ten thousand gallons per minute from fissures in the limestone forty feet below. A self-propelled, cable-guided raft with a center viewing well allows a good look down at the constantly moving water, shifting patterns in the sands, and the fat trout that appear reach-out-and-touch-them close.

Anything as stunningly beautiful and mysterious as the emerald waters of the Big Spring is bound to have a legend or several attached to it. One, on

KITCH-ITI-KIPI, THE BIG SPRING

WHAT Michigan's largest spring is at the heart of Palms Book State Park.

WHERE M-149, north of US 2 at Thompson

COST Recreation Passport required: residents, $12 annual; non-residents, $9 day pass, $34 annual

PRO TIP While viewing the underwater wonders, if you see something that looks like a cell phone, it is. Be sure to hold onto yours when taking photos.

The 388-acre park is open year-round, although in winter you may have to snowshoe, cross-country ski, or snowmobile to see the spring which, at a constant forty-five degrees, never freezes.

Kids of all ages love to pilot the raft to the center of the spring for the best view of the fish and the bottom, forty feet down.

a suspiciously familiar theme, involves a chieftain and maiden, unrequited love, and a life lost. Then there's the story of how this natural wonder came to be protected as Palms Book State Park thanks to John Bellaire, a shop owner from nearby Manistique. In the early 1920s, Bellaire found the spring overgrown and used as a rubbish dump by a nearby lumber camp. He recognized it as a treasure to be protected for public enjoyment and convinced the Palms Book Land Company to sell the spring and ninety acres to the state for ten dollars. It's said that Bellaire visited the spring almost daily. It's also said that he had a poet friend who concocted the Indian legend.

48 ART WITH A REPURPOSE

Who looks at a car hood and sees a robin's breast, or a coffee pot as a human face?

As a lad growing up in Detroit, Ritch Branstrom didn't intend to make a career of turning beer cans into fish, or car hoods into big birds. But he's now a widely known Yooper artist, captivating collectors while cleaning up the landscape by creating found object art at his adhocWORKshop in Rapid River. Always fascinated by taking things apart and building contraptions, Branstrom absorbed a lot by watching his father, a mechanic who made magic with his tools; three older brothers who were always tinkering in the garage; and uncles skilled in construction work. On family vacations Up North he grew attached to the UP, and he found his life's path studying art at Northern Michigan University in Marquette.

From his workshop in Rapid River, Branstrom uses his considerable skill with the drill and ability to see life in cast-off objects to transform silverware, vacuum cleaners, pipes, bowling pins, bottle caps, bicycle and car parts—anything imaginable—into personality-filled dogs, birds, fish, people, and critters of all sizes. His endearing, nineteen-foot-long dog *Rusty* claimed fifth place among more than 1,500 entries in the international ArtPrize competition in Grand Rapids.

ADHOCWORKSHOP

WHAT Gallery of found objects by artist Ritch Branstrom

WHERE 10495 S. Main St., Rapid River

COST Free to browse; prices start at $45 for the popular beer can fish

PRO TIP Look for Ritch's towering heron and massive mosquito perched on a boxcar on the south side of US 2, west of Rapid River.

A big bird and almost life-size UP mosquito reside at the side of US 2 between Rapid River and Gladstone.

Gallery hours are by chance or appointment; if he's not in, follow the contact instructions posted on the door and he'll likely be able to meet you there. You can take a seat on the bench in front of the shop and while away the time with a book from the Little Free Library housed in his *Rocketman Reading Robot*.

Branstrom constructed his twenty-foot *Oilspill Blue Heron* of gas tanks, oil pans, drums, and gas station columns in response to environmental damage caused by oil spills.

49 MURDER, HE WROTE

How did a fly-fishing judge bring Hollywood to his hometown?

John D. Voelker, the grandson of a German immigrant beer maker, was born in Ishpeming in 1903. The youngest of six sons, he learned from his father to love the outdoors and trout fishing. After obtaining a law degree from the University of Michigan in 1928, Voelker worked for a firm in Marquette before moving to Chicago, where he married Grace Taylor. After a few years, he'd had enough of the city and returned to the UP. He was elected Marquette County prosecutor in 1934, and through the decades he maintained a private law practice, was appointed to the Michigan Supreme Court, and served on multiple committees of the State Bar of Michigan.

In 1952, he used a temporary insanity argument to successfully defend a serviceman for murdering his wife's accused rapist. Voelker, under the pen name Robert Traver, turned the story into the national best-selling book *Anatomy of a Murder.* Otto Preminger promptly acquired the film rights and decided to shoot it on location, bringing stars James Stewart, Lee Remick, Ben Gazzara, Eve Arden, and Arthur O'Connell, as well as Duke Ellington, who wrote the jazzy musical score, to the UP. The film premiered in 1959 and has been cited by the American Bar Association as one of the great legal movies and by the American Film Institute among the top ten in the genre of classic American courtroom dramas.

Film locations include the Marquette County Courthouse and Thunder Bay Inn in Big Bay, the village where the attack and murder took place.

Voelker continued to practice law, fish, and write, notably *Trout Madness*, *Anatomy of a Fisherman*, and *Trout Magic*.

Top left: John Voelker and James Stewart light up cigars during a break in filming a courthouse scene. Photo courtesy of Northern Michigan University Archives.

Top right: John Voelker and cast during a break in filming a courthouse scene.Photo courtesy of Northern Michigan University Archives.

Above left: The Marquette County Courthouse has an exhibit about the making of the movie.

ANATOMY OF A MURDER

WHAT Self-guided tour of locations related to the trial behind the best-selling *Anatomy of a Murder* book and star-studded movie

WHERE Marquette, Ishpeming, Michigamme, and Big Bay

COST Free

PRO TIP Pick up a tour brochure from the Travel Marquette office at 117 W. Washington St., Marquette

50 SOMETHING FISHY

Why is there a shrine to Hemingway alongside the Fox River?

Northern Michigan played a big part in Ernest Hemingway's life—a lasting part, that would surface in his writing years after he'd left the state. From his birth in 1899, the Hemingway family traveled from their home in Oak Park, Illinois, to their cottage on Walloon Lake near Petoskey, in the northwest corner of Michigan's Lower Peninsula. That's where Ernie learned to love the outdoors, fishing, and hunting (and carousing). Some of these experiences showed up in his series of short pieces that form *The Nick Adams Stories*, published in 1925.

In 1919, after an injury to his leg in World War I in Italy, Hemingway returned to Michigan to heal and to write. It was then that he and a couple of buddies headed to the UP to fish near Seney, an old rough-and-tumble logging town. They hiked north to a spot on the East Branch of the Fox River, where they camped and fished. The memories of that trip are the basis of his story "Big Two-Hearted River."

From the story: "The river was there. It swirled against the log spiles of the bridge. Nick looked down into the clear, brown water, colored from the pebbly bottom, and watched the trout keeping themselves steady in the current with wavering fins."

HEMINGWAY FISHED HERE

WHAT A marker at the UP river that Hemingway really fished

WHERE State Forest Campground on M-77, seven miles north of Seney

COST Free to see, fee to camp

PRO TIP Officially, a Michigan Recreational Passport is required for entry, but unless you're staying you can probably get a quick look at the site for free. The marker is next to campsite #19.

The Fox River gave Hemingway good fishing, but he decided that the nearby Big Two-Hearted had a better name for his Nick Adams story.

There is a river in Michigan named the Big Two-Hearted, but it's miles from the site marked with the riverside plaque recently installed by the Michigan Outdoor Writers Association, which explains, "He said he borrowed the name of another Upper Peninsula river for the title because it had more poetry."

Hemingway earned rave reviews from critics for his innovative, descriptive writing style in the two-part short story "Big Two-Hearted River."

51 IF THEY COULD SEE IT NOW

Do the spirits of Fayette return to enjoy their old home town?

Stroll the remains of Fayette, a pretty, pristine ghost town on Lake Michigan's Big Bay de Noc, and you will have to dig deep to imagine the noise and commotion and the air thick with the soot and smoke of the charcoal pig iron operation that thrived here from 1867 to 1891. Now a state park, the 711-acre Fayette Historic Townsite preserves some of the homes, industrial buildings, hotel, town hall, opera house, and other structures that sheltered this community of hardy souls. In gray, weathered buildings, you get glimpses of the five hundred lives lived here and can almost feel their presence. There's the shop of D. Dupont, Barber, shaving mugs at the ready. A page from an 1876 ledger shows how much beef, at eleven cents a pound, was bought at the company store by superintendent JB Kitchen, who earned one hundred dollars monthly, and charcoal worker Edward McNally, whose salary was thirty-nine dollars. At the Shelton House hotel, the dining room was "abundantly supplied with the best this section of the planet affords." (Everything is relative; consider that "this section of the planet" is located near the end of the remote Garden Peninsula, surrounded by woods and water.)

The crystal clear Snail Shell Harbor, once a port for ore carriers, now welcomes recreational boaters to its deep

---

The state park has five miles of hiking/cross-country ski trails, plus a beach, boat launch, picnic area, modern campground, and a house that sleeps up to ten.

The Fayette Historic Townsite preserves twenty buildings; eleven have exhibits that describe the work and lives of the five hundred people who lived in this remote company town.

FAYETTE HISTORIC STATE PARK

WHAT Tour the buildings and sites of the former iron smelting town of Fayette.

WHERE At the end of M-183, 17 miles south of US 2 on the Garden Peninsula

COST Recreation Passport required: residents, $12 annual; non-residents, $9 day pass, $34 annual

PRO TIP Get oriented to Fayette with the scale model of the site at the visitor center, and pick up a map for a self-guided visit or check on times of guided tours.

blue waters. They're protected by a limestone bluff that once was quarried for the smelting process. Nearby, massive stone kilns anchor the furnace complex. It's easy to understand what the Jackson Iron Company's Fayette Brown saw in this spot, with its abundant natural resources seemingly made for an industrial town. Too bad the town folk weren't able to enjoy Fayette as tourists do today. Or, given the eerie feelings of presence that Fayette evokes, maybe they do.

52 FAMILY SECRET

Who are the people permanently camped at Van Cleve Park?

On the shore of Little Bay de Noc in Gladstone, what appears to be a Native American family of six (and pet bear!) is at home in a corner of Van Cleve Park. The history of the painted cement folk art sculptures is a bit of a mystery even to the city of Gladstone which, according to the descriptive plaque at the site, received the collection as a gift in 1988. That marker credits E. H. Levely with creating the statues around 1910 in the Lower Peninsula's Midland County. However, according to a lovely website about the history of Edenville, a town in that area, it was Alfred Henry (A. H., not E. H.) Levely (1871–1940) who was the artist, poet, and gas station owner behind the sculptures. Levely, who favored Michigan and Native American themes in his creations, displayed his works roadside, hoping to entice curious customers to stop at his business.

According to the story, the sculptures lived for a while at the Houghton Lake home of W. C. Wickham, a friend of the artist. They caught the eye of Henry Ford, who apparently tried to purchase them, but Wickham declined the offer. Wickham's son Albert moved the group to his property in Rapid River, east of Gladstone, and in 1988 relocated them to their current waterfront home.

FOLK ART STATUES

WHAT Levely folk art statues

WHERE Van Cleve Park, Gladstone

COST Free

PRO TIP Look at one of the statues and stroll back and forth to see if you feel like it is following you with its eyes.

Their backstory is uncertain, but the painted cement folk sculptures are worth a visit.

Gladstone City Manager Darcy Long admits that there is not a lot of solid information about the history of the sculptures, but he says that the city appreciates their worth and is committed to preserving them.

53 WHITE PINE WORTH A MINT

What UP landmark rocks Michigan's America the Beautiful quarter?

French fur trader Pierre-Esprit Radisson was the first documented visitor to describe the Pictured Rocks, the multicolored, mineral-stained sandstone cliffs that stretch for fifteen miles and tower two hundred feet above the Lake Superior shoreline. Of his 1658 impression, Radisson recorded, "Nature has made it pleasant to the eye, the spirit, and the belly." He wrote that the Indians who accompanied the expedition left an offering of tobacco at the rocks to the spirit they called Nauitouchsinagoit, "the likeness of the devil."

A member of an 1840 expedition led by Michigan's state geologist Douglass Houghton was especially wowed by Chapel Rock. He said, "Among the characteristic features, none is more extra-ordinary than one to which the French voyageurs have appropriately given the name of *La Chapelle*. The span of this arch is thirty-two feet, as viewed from the water, in which direction the spectator looks completely through the temple into the woodland beyond. The strength of the roof thus upheld must be considerable, since it is clothed with timber, and from the very center shoots, spire-like, a lofty pine."

Pictured Rocks are colored by streaks of minerals that ooze from cracks: the red and orange come from iron; blue and green, copper; brown and black, manganese; and white, limonite.

Chapel Rock has inspired admiration and fear in the Ojibway, French voyageurs, explorers, geologists, and tourists.

CHAPEL ROCK

WHAT A tree that defies the odds and stands strong on a rock outcropping on Lake Superior

WHERE Pictured Rocks National Lakeshore

COST Free to hike; fee for boat tour

PRO TIP View Pictured Rocks on a two-to-three-hour boat tour from Munising, or hike the three-mile trail to see Chapel Rock and Chapel Falls.

The rock arch that once joined Chapel Rock to the mainland has crumbled, but the spire-like, lofty white pine remains connected by its root system. The distinctive formation was chosen in 2018 to represent Michigan in the National Park Quarters series. Designated in 1966 as the first National Lakeshore in the system, Pictured Rocks is accessible from Grand Marais at the eastern end and Munising to the west.

54 INVENTOR OF THE OUTDOORS

Who is the entrepreneur that made Gladstone the outdoor equipment capital of the world in the early 1900s?

As a surveyor and timber cruiser—someone who traipses through the woods to assess stands of lumber—Webster L. Marble (1854–1930) found the tools he relied on in the wilderness to be inferior, if not nonexistent. Marble began turning his ideas into prototypes at his home workshop in Gladstone, and in 1892 he manufactured his first invention, a universal rifle sight. By 1898 he had patented his safety pocket axe and formed the Marble Safety Axe Company.

At the turn of the twentieth century, Americans who'd moved from rural to urban areas were discovering the recreational appeal of the great outdoors, and Marble found an audience for his growing line of sturdy and practical tools and gear. A pin-on compass that fastened to clothing. A waterproof matchbox. Strong but lightweight hunting knives, and six-blade knives for Boy Scouts and Girl Scouts. His popular Game Getter combination gun with folding stock could be used for small or large game.

WEBSTER MARBLE MUSEUM

WHAT Tribute to the inventor of multiple tools and gear designed for outdoor recreation

WHERE State Fairgrounds, N. Lincoln Rd. & Ninth Ave. N., Escanaba

COST Free; donations accepted

PRO TIP Pick up tips on other things to see and do in the area; the museum is part of the Visit Escanaba Welcome Center.

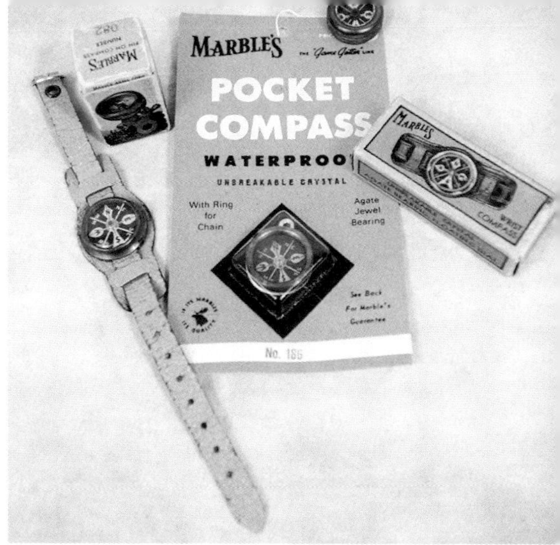

Left: After falling into the Sturgeon River, Marble was inspired to invent the waterproof match safe. Photo courtesy of Michigan History Center.

Right: Webster Marble developed a waterproof compass with an unbreakable crystal. Photo courtesy of Michigan History Center.

Importantly, Marble was also a master marketer, utilizing testimonials in advertising, romanticized images of outdoor scenes, and promotional product placement to great effect. Theodore Roosevelt carried Marble compasses on his dangerous 1913 expedition into the Brazilian wilderness, and in 1927 Charles Lindbergh, on his solo transatlantic flight, packed Marble's knife, compass, and match safe.

The Webster Marble Museum tells the story of the entrepreneur who held more than sixty patents for "Marble's Outing Equipment." Most of the items displayed were donated by Dennis Pace, who collected Marble materials for four decades.

Marble Arms still supplies sights for most American gunmakers. According to the company website, "As always, Marble's products are all steel, all American, and all Gladstone, Michigan U.S.A."

55 DRY HUMOR

What's a guy to do with his free time when he gives up drinking beer?

Tom Lakenen is a hard worker. Has been since he became a pipefitter, fresh out of high school with a welding class under his belt. He moved from the pipefitters' to the boilermakers' union, where he works construction as a welder. After a day on the job, he'd kick back with a beer or a dozen. In the late 1990s, Lakenen quit drinking, and with the extra hours he had on his beer-free hands, he put his welding skills to work creating sculptures of scrap metal carted home from job sites. With no training as an artist, he found he had a talent for it and displayed his whimsical art in the front yard of his Marquette-area residence. It got thumbs-ups from passersby, but it rankled local government officials who classified his quirky and colorful creations as signage that had to go.

LAKENENLAND SCULPTURE PARK

WHAT Display of Tom Lakenen's Junkyard Art on thirty-seven wooded acres

WHERE M-28, 15 miles east of Marquette

COST Free; donations accepted

PRO TIP Located on snowmobile trail #417, it's a popular destination for sledders, and it's a viewing spot for the UP200 Dog Sled Race each February.

Lakenen moved them to his backyard, which, before long, was overpopulated. Out of space and frustrated that he couldn't share his art with anyone but his family, he envisioned a sculpture park open to the public. In 2003 he and his wife, Lisa, refinanced their home to purchase thirty-seven acres along the highway between Marquette and Munising and named it Lakenenland. He relocated his sculptures, cut trails through the woods, added a fire pit, put snacks in a cabinet, and invited anyone at any time, all year-round, free of charge

In his spare time, welder Tom Lakenen creates sculptures from scrap metal that he plants in his free park on the highway between Munising and Marquette.

(he accepts donations). Over the years he's added outhouses, a stage, a pond, and a nifty pavilion with a massive stone fireplace. His woods are now home to more than one hundred sculptures that honor miners and lumberjacks, salute the military, make political statements, or are just goofy. There are monsters, aliens, dinosaurs, and critters of all kinds that are, as he describes, "All the things I saw while drinking."

Lakenenland will remain free to see; Lakenen doesn't want anyone to stay away because they cannot afford to pay an admission.

56 SECRET SAUSAGE

What Italian specialty is found only in the iron mining areas of the UP?

An Italian specialty that Yoopers know and love as cudighi is little known elsewhere—even in other parts of Michigan and its northern Italian homeland. The sweetly spiced pork sausage was brought to the UP by immigrants who came to work the iron mines and is popular in the Iron Mountain and Marquette County areas. Cudighi (pronounced coo-dig-ee or cud-i-gee) may have roots in the Cotechino Modena sausage. The American version comes in mild, medium, and hot varieties and has a uniquely and subtly sweet flavor that varies by kitchen. Generally, it involves combinations of cinnamon, cloves, nutmeg, allspice, and garlic (of course), and sometimes fennel, red wine, and—well, it's a secret.

Food history records show that *gudighi* was introduced to Yoopers at a sandwich stand in 1936 and consisted of the homemade sausage topped with chopped onions, ketchup, and mustard. After World War II, the specialty's name became *cudighi* and the sandwich evolved to what is known today: the sausage flattened into a patty and fried on a flat-top (like a burger) and dressed with the original onions, mustard, and ketchup, but with mozzarella cheese and pizza sauce added. The messy combo is served on a roll substantial enough to handle the deliciousness.

CUDIGHI

WHAT Spicy yet sweet northern Italian sausage found almost exclusively in the UP

WHERE At restaurants and markets in and around Iron Mountain and Marquette County

COST Sandwiches are about $7

PRO TIP Try the homemade cudighi-topped pie at Congress Pizza in Ishpeming.

A cudighi sandwich is the specialty of the house at Ralph's Italian Deli in Ishpeming.

The sausage may have been forgotten in Italy, but it's celebrated at the annual Cudighi Cook-Off in the old mining town of Ishpeming, west of Marquette.

57 ICE HIKE

What UP caves can you explore only during the winter months?

The Rock River Canyon Ice Caves are a natural wonder found in the Rock River Canyon Wilderness, an area of approximately 4,700 acres within the Hiawatha National Forest. They're not actually caves, but vertical sheets of ice that form when water seeps through bedrock and melting snow runs over the small cliff. As this mix freezes, it forms curtains of ice that resemble a frozen waterfall. Behind the walls of ice formations there are cavities, or hollow areas, that can be entered and explored. Commonly known as the Eben Ice Caves for their proximity to the village of Eben Junction, they usually form in mid-to-late winter.

Reaching the caves requires a hike of almost a mile from the parking area, which is on private land. Fortunately, the owners allow visitors to park on their property and also hike across their field in order to reach the public wilderness area. Given the popularity of the caves, the snow on the hiking route is usually packed down and can be slippery. Cleats and trekking poles are recommended for walking across the wide-open field and along the wooded trail—especially at a couple of hilly spots as you approach the caves—and within the caves.

EBEN ICE CAVES

WHAT Spectacular ice formations that form cave-like areas to explore

WHERE Between Marquette and Munising; find directions at the Eben Ice Caves Facebook page.

COST Free

PRO TIP Watch the weather conditions that might affect the stability and safety of the ice caves; temperature changes can cause melting and the risk of falling ice.

The ice has yellow, green, and blue hues. Photo courtesy of Loose Canon Photography.

The Eben Ice Caves are not to be confused with the frozen formations along Lake Superior at Grand Island, the Pictured Rocks, and waterfalls, which attract ice climbers from around the world.

58 OH, CHRISTMAS TREES

Where did the ill-fated voyage of the legendary Christmas Tree Ship begin?

In the late 1800s and early 1900s, in advance of each Christmas season, schooners loaded with evergreens would set sail from the north woods, bound for cities around the Great Lakes. One of these, the three-masted *Rouse Simmons*, met a tragic end that is remembered in story and song. Captained by the experienced, respected Herman Schuenemann, the 123-foot vessel usually transported lumber, but it made an annual voyage to Chicago to sell Christmas trees harvested from the UP.

Each year a crowd gathered at the Clark Street docks on the Chicago River in eager anticipation of the arrival of "Captain Santa" and the Christmas Tree Ship.

THE CHRISTMAS TREE SHIP

WHAT Commemorative marker at the site of the harbor where the *Rouse Simmons* departed

WHERE Off US 2, Thompson, about five miles west of Manistique

COST Free

PRO TIP The US Coast Guard Cutter *Mackinaw* carries on the tradition, bringing trees from Michigan for distribution by the nonprofit organization Chicago's Christmas Ship.

In October 1971 Milwaukee scuba diver Gordon Kent Bellrichard, searching for a different ship in the Lake Michigan waters near Two Rivers, discovered the wreck of the *Rouse Simmons.*

Tranquil today, this spot was a busy lumbering center when the Christmas Tree Ship sailed out on its last voyage.

On November 22, 1912, the *Rouse Simmons* set sail from Thompson Harbor on Lake Michigan, carrying an estimated five thousand trees. The next day, the schooner went down in a snowstorm near Two Rivers, Wisconsin. At least eleven perished, but the number on board may have been more. (Tragically, Herman's older brother August Schuenemann had disappeared with his Christmas ship in a similar storm in 1898.)

A year after the loss of her husband, Barbara Schuenemann and their three daughters, Elsie and twins Hazel and Pearl, decided to carry on the family tradition, bringing Christmas trees to Chicago—eventually by train—until the mid-1930s.

59 TAKE THE HIGH ROAD

Where can you drive the highest roadway between the Rocky and Allegheny Mountains?

Winding its way for nearly ten miles along the Keweenaw Peninsula, Brockway Mountain Drive is a lasting legacy of the federally funded, Depression-era works programs. Construction of a road had been proposed in the 1920s, but it wasn't until 1933 that the Keweenaw County Road Commission launched the project, at the same time the Keweenaw Mountain Lodge was being built. The roadwork provided jobs for three hundred idled copper miners who, for a wage of twenty-five cents per hour, built the two-lane highway as well as low stone walls along the route to the summit 726 feet above Lake Superior. Unobstructed views from the top sweep across thousands of wooded acres—especially spectacular in autumn—inland lakes, rocky cliffs, Lake Superior, and, on a clear day, Isle Royale some fifty miles distant.

During spring migration tens of thousands of hawks, eagles, vultures, owls, falcons, and other birds pass through what is now a part of the 4,500-acre Keweenaw Coastal Wildlife Corridor. The Michigan Nature Association, Michigan Audubon Society, and Eagle Harbor Township have been piecing together tracts of land to create sanctuaries to protect

BROCKWAY MOUNTAIN DRIVE

WHAT Two-lane drive along the Keweenaw Peninsula to a panoramic view 726 feet above Lake Superior

WHERE Access the drive from M-26 at Eagle Harbor to the west or Copper Harbor to the east.

COST Free

PRO TIP Make it a leisurely drive. Bring binoculars, take your time, and stop at the designated scenic overlooks.

Rugged cliffs overlook miles of wilderness from the summit of Brockway Mountain Drive.

Inset: Stop at the lookout for a view of Copper Harbor, Michigan's most northern community.

the wildlife habitat and vegetation, including orchids, among the seven hundred species of wildflowers. With no light pollution, Brockway Mountain's dark skies are excellent for stargazing and, if you're lucky, catching the Northern Lights.

From its official opening in 1935, Brockway Mountain Drive was a popular destination for the motoring public and put the Keweenaw Peninsula on the tourism map.

60 THE BAND PLAYS ON

Where will you find a community band that is municipally funded, like other important city services?

Each summer Wednesday evening, forty or so musicians don their crisp white shirts, white dress jackets, black bowties, and black pants or skirts, tune up their instruments, and take the stage at Escanaba's Ludington Park. It's a tradition that dates to 1924, when the Escanaba Municipal Band was first funded "by a voter referendum." That tax assessment put the musical organization on par with other departments that are the responsibility of the city for the well-being of its citizens.

The ability for communities to levy a tax "for the maintenance and employment of a band for musical purposes" dates to 1921 and a successful campaign in Iowa led by famous bandmaster and composer Karl King. That the Iowa Band Law was quickly adopted in thirty-three states, including Michigan, is evidence of how important city bands were to the fabric of community

ESCANABA CITY BAND

WHAT A municipally funded band offering free concerts since 1924. Performances start at 7:30 p.m. on Wednesdays from June to August.

WHERE Ludington Park, Escanaba

COST Free

PRO TIP Spread a blanket and enjoy a picnic on the lawn with the music wafting from the Karas Memorial Band Shell.

The band strikes up Sousa marches and patriotic tunes, as well as Broadway and movie music, fifties favorites, jazz standards, Dixieland, and Paul Simon, Stevie Wonder, and Beatles hits.

Snappy red uniforms and military-style caps make an impression when the Escanaba City Band marches in local Fourth of July and Labor Day parades. Photos courtesy of Escanaba City Band.

life across the land. A 1926 editorial in the *Escanaba Daily Press* encouraged citizens to renew the local tax and noted, "It can be safely said that no single undertaking of past years has returned the measure of genuine pleasure to the greatest number of people, than has the municipal band in this city."

Now named the Escanaba City Band, its musicians are male, female, young, and mature. And it is still a city department supported with municipal funds that provide, as that 1926 editorial proclaimed, "the people of Escanaba with a most delightful source of amusement."

61 STUMP PRAIRIE

What great swath of desolate land inspired a novel by a Michigan writer?

The contrast is jaw-dropping. Just south of the beauty of Pictured Rocks National Lakeshore, with its brilliant rock formations, waterfalls, deep woods, and sandy beaches along majestic Lake Superior, there's an eerie landscape of jagged tree stumps, the ground covered with lichens and dotted with scrubby trees and shrubs. Kingston Plains, the area west of Grand Marais and south of Grand Sable Dunes was, until the late 1800s, thick with old-growth white pine forests. In 1882 a logging operation headed by Thomas G. Sullivan moved in, and in three years it cut fifty million feet of white pine in this area alone. By 1909 more than three thousand acres had been cleared, leaving the land strewn with slash—the scraps that had no value. The resin-filled brush burned many times, and likely raged so hot that the

KINGSTON PLAINS

WHAT Vast, eerie landscape of stump-littered land

WHERE Adams Truck Trail two miles east of H-58, southwest of Grand Marais

COST Free

PRO TIP After a sobering visit to the plains, head to Grand Marais and the Lake Superior Brewing Company; it was known as the Dunes Saloon when Jim Harrison drank there.

"The main feature of the Kingston Plains was the thousands of white pine stumps, some of them very large, which had been cut at waist or chest height . . . " from *True North* by Jim Harrison.

There's a strange beauty to the Kingston Plains, the decimated forest land struggling for rebirth.

fires cooked the sandy soil, destroying what little chance of forest revival there may have been. The most desolate area of Kingston Plains is within a couple of miles of H-58; further east along Adams Truck Trail there is more vegetation, although there are still thousands of jagged stumps among the new growth.

On a still day, the silence is as vast as the plains, and invites contemplation. Writer Jim Harrison, who was born and lived in the northern Lower Peninsula, would retreat to his cabin near Grand Marais and walk for hours across the Kingston Plains to clear his mind. The ravaged landscape is talked about in his novel *True North*, about a timber family who grew wealthy on the white pine they logged.

62 A BRIDGE TOO FAR

Got gephyrophobia?

It's of no consequence to gephyrophobiacs—those who have a fear of bridges—that the five-mile, twin-towered suspension Mackinac Bridge linking Michigan's Upper and Lower Peninsulas is a graceful engineering marvel, declared "a poem in steel" by its designer Dr. David B. Steinman (not that he was biased . . .). However majestic, practical, and structurally sound the span may be, driving over the Straits of Mackinac, where the Great Lakes Huron and Michigan mingle, is on the NOT To Do List of many people. The Mackinac Bridge Authority understands and has employees who will take the wheel of any type of vehicle and shuttle passengers across. Although it will not eliminate the fear, this free service is an option for anyone who wants to travel between the peninsulas without having to follow the land route around Lake Michigan through Wisconsin.

Until the Mighty Mac opened in November of 1957, ferries carried travelers and their vehicles across the straits. A bridge was first proposed back in 1884, a year after the opening of the Brooklyn Bridge, but half a century passed before the Mackinac Straits Bridge Authority was established in 1934 and feasibility studies began. Finally, after delays due to wars, supply shortages, and financing issues, construction on what was then the world's longest suspension bridge began in May of 1954. With towers that reach 552 feet above

---

Phone 906-643-7600, 24/7 for the driver assist service. Pedestrians, bicyclists, and snowmobilers must be transported; there is a small fee for this service, available 8 a.m.–8 p.m. daily.

Each Labor Day, thousands of pedestrians participate in the annual bridge walk, the only time that the Mackinac Bridge is closed to vehicle traffic.

often turbulent, deep waters, it boggles the mind to think about the quantity of materials and equipment, the size of the labor force, and the planning and construction methods required to erect the massive structure. An average of eleven thousand drivers make the crossing each day, taking in spectacular views of the waterway a couple of hundred feet below. It's good to know that those nervous about the bridge don't have to drive it with their eyes closed.

MACKINAC BRIDGE

WHAT The suspension bridge connecting Michigan's two peninsulas

WHERE St. Ignace in the UP; Mackinaw City in the Lower Peninsula

COST Passenger vehicles, $4; others, $5 per axle

PRO TIP Find the bridge history, facts, construction photos, and more at mackinacbridge.org.

63 PORCH APPEAL

Is it worth a ten-spot to sit in this spot?

From the day it opened in July of 1887, the pillar-lined porch of Mackinac Island's Grand Hotel was the place to be, for catching cool breezes off the Straits of Mackinac, enjoying live musical performances, and whiling away the hours in conversation or with a book. It was a "flirtation walk" for couples and a promenade for those who wanted to see and be seen. There were demonstrations of the new invention called the Edison phonograph, and in the 1930s the porch was a showcase for the Chrysler Corporation's new line of cars—despite Mackinac Island's ban on motor vehicles. Dignitaries welcomed there include Presidents Truman, Kennedy, Ford, Clinton, and George H. W. Bush, as well as Arnold Palmer, Rosemary Clooney, James Earl Jones, and Mark Twain.

Ripley's Believe It or Not declared the porch, at 880 feet, to be the world's longest. Grand Hotel still claims that distinction, but at the actual measurement of "just" 660 feet. As in two football fields. An eighth of a mile. Nearly as long as Detroit's seventy-three-story Renaissance Center is tall. Grand Hotel, which was built of mountains of white pine in just ninety days, was one of more than 1,200 wood-frame hotels that offered Gilded Age patrons respite from the heat of the city. It is one of only twelve or so remaining, and it has been owned and operated by the Musser family for nearly ninety years. Guests enjoy traditions such as afternoon tea, croquet on the lawn, dressing for dinner, dancing to an orchestra, and, of course, relaxing on the flag-bedecked porch, trimmed with Grand Hotel's signature red geraniums and furnished with one hundred white rocking chairs for enjoying the view, a beverage, or a nap. Porch appeal is so great that non-hotel guests are willing to pay a ten-dollar fee to stroll, sit, and soak in the history of the place.

Left: Christopher Reeve chats with media on the porch of Grand Hotel during a break in filming Somewhere in Time. *Photo courtesy of Grand Hotel.*

Right: The view from Grand Hotel's porch takes in the Straits of Mackinac and passing freighter traffic.

GRAND HOTEL PORCH

WHAT The longest porch in the world at one of the last great wooden resort hotels

WHERE Grand Hotel, Mackinac Island

COST $10 for non-hotel guests

PRO TIP The fee also allows access to the gardens and public spaces and may be applied to the price of the hotel's Grand Luncheon Buffet.

As the staff cleans out the pantry and wine cellar at season's end, "Close the Grand" overnight guests enjoy casual meals and help haul rocking chairs off the porch for winter storage.

64 FUDGE FACTOR

How did tiny Mackinac Island become known as America's Fudge Capital?

For over a century, freshly made fudge has been the souvenir most identified with Mackinac Island, the Victorian-era resort destination in the waters between the Upper and Lower Peninsulas. Tourists are so taken with fudge that on a busy summer day they consume or purchase ten thousand pounds of the confection, earning them the nickname "fudgies." The fudge phenomenon dates to 1887, when sail maker Henry Murdick and his son Jerome were hired by Grand Hotel to make awnings for the new resort. Seeing the potential in the blossoming tourism industry, Henry carried on the family's main trade while Jerome took his mother Sara's fudge recipe and opened Murdick's Candy Kitchen, the first such confectionery shop on the island.

Jerome didn't just make fudge—he enticed visitors with an entertaining show by cooking the candy in the front of the shop where they could watch the process. That tradition continues today at multiple stores, where candymakers hand stir their special combinations of sugar, cream, butter, chocolate, and flavorings in copper kettles, then cool and paddle the mix into shape on marble-topped tables, where the long loaves are sliced into half-pound slabs. Gimmicks designed to drum up sales include the use of fans to push the irresistible scent of fudge onto the streets and samples

---

Fudge wars shook genteel Mackinac Island in the 1960s when Detroit candy man Harry Ryba arrived with aggressive marketing techniques that led to a lawsuit. He lost that battle, but the business thrives.

Mackinac Island candymakers concoct dozens of flavors of fudge and sell up to ten thousand pounds of it on a typical summer day.

MACKINAC ISLAND FUDGE

WHAT The signature souvenir for tourists since 1887

WHERE Multiple locations, mostly on Main St., Mackinac Island

COST About $8 per half-pound slab; multiple slices usually discounted

PRO TIP Try before you buy; free samples abound.

freely offered at sweet shops operated by seven candymakers. In addition to Murdick's, Grand Hotel, Joann's Fudge, May's Candy, Murray Hotel Fudge Company, Ryba's Fudge Shop, and Sanders Candy offer fudge on Mackinac. You won't have trouble finding them—just follow the aroma.

65 LASTING IMPRESSIONS

Where did the "father of wildlife ecology" spend the formative summers of his youth?

At the eastern end of the UP, stretching twelve miles along Lake Huron, the low-key Les Cheneaux area has been a summertime resort destination for well over a century. In 1898 Carl Leopold of Burlington, Iowa, bought a cottage on Marquette Island, the largest of the thirty-six islands of the glacier-formed archipelago. Each summer, he and his family enjoyed the natural beauty of its rocky shores, marshes, meadows, woodlands, and protected bays.

Aldo, oldest of the four Leopold children, spent hours exploring the woods and waters of Les Cheneaux (French for "the channels"). Frederick said of his brother, "Aldo knew most of the island intimately. He produced several handmade maps artistically decorated and illustrated with typical trees, animals, and birds in appropriate places. All of the trails were shown including some newer trails which he himself created."

ALDO LEOPOLD AND LES CHENEAUX

WHAT Les Cheneaux Islands, which undoubtedly influenced the lad who became known for his views on conservation

WHERE M-134 along Lake Huron, Eastern UP

COST Free; fee for Aldo Leopold Festival activities

PRO TIP Access to the islands is by watercraft; kayak and canoe rentals are available in the village of Hessel.

In 1993 The Nature Conservancy designated the northern shore of Lake Huron one of the "Last Great Places" on earth.

Future conservationist Aldo Leopold spent weeks each summer exploring Marquette Island. Photo courtesy of TM Peterson/Little Traverse Conservancy.

Aldo Leopold graduated from the Yale Forest School in 1909 but continued to visit Les Cheneaux even after he went to work for the new US Forest Service in Arizona and New Mexico. In 1924 his work took him to Wisconsin, where his philosophy of conservation, wildlife and game management, and ecological restoration evolved.

Leopold died in 1948. The following year his collection of essays, *A Sand County Almanac*, was published; it has since sold more than two million copies. Many consider him the most influential conservation thinker of the twentieth century.

Several initiatives in recent years recognize Aldo Leopold, his accomplishments, and his connection to Les Cheneaux: a Michigan state historical marker was installed on the Lake Huron shore; an annual Aldo Leopold Festival features guided nature hikes, birding, paddling, and presentations; and the Little Traverse Conservancy established the 1,683-acre Aldo Leopold Nature Preserve on Marquette Island, which had been the playground of the future "Father of Wildlife Ecology."

66 NIGHT MOVES

Who goes rockhounding in the dark?

Erik Rintamaki still has the rock that he says sparked his lifelong fascination with picking. He was an infant on his first rockhounding excursion with his dad, and his mom painted the specimen as a memento. Rintamaki is a gem and mineral dealer from Brimley, a speck of a town conveniently located near the rock-strewn beaches of Lake Superior. He's made a lot of fantastic finds in his lifelong quest for unusual specimens, but nothing compares to his discovery in the summer of 2017. Hoping to uncover fluorescing agates, Rintamaki purchased an inexpensive longwave UV flashlight and headed to the shore in the dark. He was rewarded with two tiny, glowing rocks. After some frustrating efforts to find more of the unusual specimens, he upgraded to a better quality of black light, met with greater success, and realized he'd discovered something special. He sent some to be analyzed by the experts at Michigan Tech University and the University of Saskatchewan, who confirmed that he had found "syenite clasts containing fluorescent sodalite"—the first documented in the state. This sodalite is not believed to be native to Michigan but is thought to have been pushed south from Canada by way of Lake Superior.

YOOPERLITE EXPERIENCE

WHAT Guided, two-hour night picking excursion to find glowing rocks on the Lake Superior shore

WHERE Outings depart from three locations in the Eastern UP, depending on date selected.

COST $150; includes a UV light with rechargeable batteries and charger and all the Yooperlites you find (up to the state limited maximum of twenty-five pounds annually).

PRO TIP At the Yooperlites website, Rintamaki shares tips for a self-guided rock-picking trip.

Yooperlites look like plain gray rocks by day, but they take on a bright orange glow under a high-quality UV light. Photos courtesy of Yooperlite Experience.

To the naked eye they appear as plain gray rocks, but they show a brilliant, eerie flash of orange under black light. Rintamaki registered them as "Yooperlites," and he has attracted international attention for his discovery. He sells Yooperlites at his website and offers guided, nighttime excursions to prime picking sites, promising that there's nothing like the thrill of discovering the distinctive flash of orange on your own.

"The only way to see the magic of these stones is to discover them on your own. It's not a tour, it's an experience." —Erik Rintamaki

67 BEAR NECESSITIES

Where do abandoned and abused black bears find refuge in the UP?

On 240 acres not far from Tahquamenon Falls, black bears roam in the safety of the largest such refuge in the United States. They receive food and care in a natural environment designed to protect them as they grow or while recuperating from an injury. Oswald's Bear Ranch is the permanent home to orphaned cubs that are rescued before they are able to learn how to survive on their own. It's also a rehab facility for older, injured bears that are released back into the wilds when they are healthy enough. At any time there are usually about forty bears at the ranch, which has been a wildly popular visitor attraction since it opened to the public in 1997.

Prior to that, Dean Oswald, a former firefighter from the Lower Peninsula, had kept rescued cubs at the retirement property he and his wife, Jewel, moved to in 1984. Word about his passion for the animals got out, bears continued to arrive, and the refuge grew. Oswald built fenced enclosures to keep the males, females, and yearlings in separate areas. He added walking paths and a raised viewing platform at each habitat for better photo ops of bears eating, roaming, sleeping, and lumbering around. Oswald has built a reputation that attracts bears from

OSWALD'S BEAR RANCH

WHAT The largest refuge in the United States dedicated to black bears

WHERE 13814 County Rd. 407, Newberry

COST Individuals, $10; vehicles, $20; photos, $10 per group (cash)

PRO TIP Plan to catch the bear frenzy at feeding time, which is at 4 p.m. daily.

A popular attraction is the photo booth, where you can have pictures taken, using your camera, with a bear cub (separate fee charged).

everywhere: in late 2018 when a sow black bear at Grand Teton National Park had to be euthanized, her two cubs were relocated to the UP.

Photo and admission fees and donations support the private operation and make possible the addition of an adjacent two hundred acres dedicated to a sanctuary for bears to live in a protected habitat not open to public view.

Resting in peace at the Bear Cemetery is the beloved Tyson, who weighed in at one thousand pounds and was declared America's largest black bear before he died at age twelve in July of 2000.

68 TIME TESTED

Where will you find four of Michigan's oldest standing structures?

Human history at Mackinac Island, where Lakes Huron and Michigan meet, reaches back centuries as a sacred gathering place and burial ground for the Anishnaabek-Ojibwa people. In the 1600s the French explorers, missionaries, voyageurs, and fur traders arrived. In 1780 the British established Fort Mackinac on a bluff 150 feet above the Straits of Mackinac, and from 1796 through the War of 1812, they fought with the Americans for control of the strategic location. The whitewashed stone walls of Fort Mackinac contain Michigan's oldest standing building, the Officer's Stone Quarters, an original fort structure dating to 1780. It now serves as the Fort Mackinac Tea Room, where you can enjoy lunch or a beverage with spectacular views of the straits. The fort's 1828 Post Hospital is the oldest standing hospital building in Michigan,

MACKINAC STATE HISTORIC PARKS BUILDINGS

WHAT Original structures at the 1780 Fort Mackinac and Historic Downtown Mackinac

WHERE Mackinac Island

COST Adults, $13.50; youth, $8; four and under, free

PRO TIP Admission to the fort includes entry to the park's Historic Downtown Mackinac sites, Biddle House and Mackinac Island Native American Museum, and Richard & Jane Manoogian Mackinac Art Museum.

Fort Mackinac is a living history museum with demonstrations and tours about military and civilian life led by costumed interpreters at various times throughout each day.

Mackinac Island is home to several of Michigan's oldest standing structures, including fort buildings and Mission Church.

and its exhibit explains medical care at the military outpost and nineteenth-century medical practices.

The park's three Historic Downtown Mackinac sites include the McGulpin House, Michigan's oldest residential structure. Mission Church, the oldest church building in the state, dates to 1829 and is the earliest surviving New England-style church in the Midwest.

69 FROM CENTER FOR PEACE TO PEACEFUL RETREAT

How did a defunct campus become an award-winning resort?

At the eastern end of Mackinac Island, the red-roofed buildings of Mission Point Resort sprawl across eighteen waterfront acres at the spot where French missionaries landed in 1634. Nearby, the Protestant Mission House school was built in 1825, followed by Mission Church in 1829. The history of the low-slung gleaming white compound at Mission Point that now welcomes guests as a full-service resort began in the 1950s as a center for members of Moral Re-Armament (MRA), an international peace movement. MRA was launched by an American in Europe in 1938 and was rooted in the belief that the world needed a moral and spiritual, not strictly a military, solution to world problems.

MISSION POINT RESORT

WHAT Full-service resort at the eastern end of Mackinac Island

WHERE One Lakeshore Dr., Mackinac Island

COST $225 per night and up for a variety of accommodations; specials available

PRO TIP Bring a book or just watch Lake Huron and passing boat traffic from an Adirondack chair on the Great Lawn.

Followers of the pacifist organization first assembled on Mackinac Island in 1942 and in 1955 began construction on a permanent conference center. The MRA started with an eight-hundred-seat theater, followed in 1956 by its great hall and residences. By 1965, after the

Left: The resort offers garden and history tours, as well as croquet and bocce ball on the manicured lawn and other recreational pursuits.

Right: The Mission Point Resort lobby, with wood-burning fireplaces and a soaring ceiling supported by massive, fifty-foot pine beam trusses, was built in 1956 as the MRA great hall.

deaths of MRA leaders, the facility was converted to Mackinac College. The liberal arts school graduated only one class, in 1970. In its next life the campus was known as the Mackinac Hotel and Conference Center, and in the late 1980s it was named Mission Point Resort. Since 2015, when the Ware family purchased the property, it has benefited from major investment, including complete refurbishment of all 241 guest rooms and suites. With the amenities of its Lakeside Spa, yoga space by the water's edge on the Great Lawn, and garden meditation spots, Mission Point is contributing in its own way to a more peaceful world from its spot on the sunrise side of Mackinac Island.

Mission Point offers informative walking tours with the resort's historian and tours of the award-winning gardens with the resident horticulturalist.

70 THE LEGENDS LIVE ON

Where can you learn about the power, majesty, and tragedies of the great freshwater seas?

The light tower at Whitefish Point, a navigational beacon for Lake Superior traffic since 1861, is the oldest operational light on the big lake. It stands at the eastern end of the Shipwreck Coast, so named for the number of vessels that have gone down along the eighty-mile stretch westward. Those waters are the resting place of more than two hundred of the 550 known ships lost in all of Lake Superior, including the infamous *Edmund Fitzgerald*. The 729-foot ore carrier went down in a vicious storm on November 10, 1975, just seventeen miles off Whitefish Point. There's no better place for the Great Lakes Shipwreck Museum, which explores the lives and lore of the inland seas.

It's easy to spend the better part of a day at the compound of tidy white buildings on the site of a former US Coast Guard Station. A highlight of the main museum exhibits, which describe a number of wrecks, is the bell from the *Edmund Fitzgerald*, retrieved in 1995 from the Lake Superior depth of 535 feet. (The bell was replaced with a replica bearing the names of all twenty-nine lost.) The Surfboat House and USCG Motor Lifeboat House display the types of boats that were

---

The legend lives on from the Chippewa on down
Of the big lake they called "gitche gumee"
The lake, it is said, never gives up her dead
When the skies of November turn gloomy . . .

—From Gordon Lightfoot's 1976 ballad, "The Wreck of the Edmund Fitzgerald"

Learn about lives and vessels lost, and those who work to save them, at the multibuilding museum at Whitefish Point on Lake Superior. Top photo courtesy of Great Lakes Shipwreck Historical Society.

GREAT LAKES SHIPWRECK MUSEUM

WHAT Comprehensive exhibits about Great Lakes sailors and ships in several buildings on the shore of Lake Superior

WHERE 18335 N. Whitefish Point Rd., about 11 miles north of Paradise

COST Adults, $13; youth, $9; discounted family ticket available

PRO TIP Plan well ahead for an overnight stay in the 1923 Coast Guard Lifeboat Station Crews Quarters; the five rooms are booked well in advance.

used in lifesaving efforts, and a 1920s US Navy building houses changing exhibits. The Lightkeepers Quarters offers a glimpse of the lonely life at the outpost, and visitors may climb the light tower for a small additional fee. Watch the video in the theater and follow the boardwalk to the Lake Superior shoreline, where you might catch sight of a passing freighter.

71 SOO VIEW

What Brutalist tower was built as a Shrine of the Missionaries in Michigan's oldest city?

It's not the tallest structure in the UP, but it's up there, and its architecture is hard to miss. Sault Ste. Marie's 210-foot Tower of History was built in 1968, when the geometric, reinforced-concrete style known as Brutalism was hot. Standing in stark contrast next to the graceful spire of the Gothic Revival Holy Name of Mary Catholic Church, the modern observation tower/museum was supposed to be phase one of a compound that would have included a new church building. The development stopped at phase one, and the tower was given to Sault Historic Sites to operate as one of its attractions, which include the freighter turned Museum Ship *Valley Camp*, historic homes, and River of History museum.

Visitors can climb the 292 steps to the top of the tower or opt for an elevator ride to the observation platforms with views of the St. Marys River, boat traffic through the Soo Locks, the International Bridge connecting the twin Canadian City of Sault Ste. Marie, Ontario, and the forested wilderness beyond. Museum exhibits pay homage to the missionaries, as intended, but also touch on Native American and other local history.

The church structure, built in 1881, is the fifth to house Michigan's oldest Catholic church, which was established by Jesuit missionaries in 1668.

TOWER OF HISTORY

WHAT On a clear day, enjoy miles-wide views of the Soo Locks and Canadian wilderness.

WHERE 501 E. Water St., Sault Ste. Marie

COST Adults, $7.50; children, $3.75

PRO TIP Buy a combination ticket with one or two other Sault Historic Sites and soak up Soo history at a savings.

This example of the Brutalism architectural movement contrasts sharply with that of St. Mary's, the first cathedral of the Diocese of Marquette. Photo courtesy of Sault Historic Sites.

The Tower of History opened three hundred years after the founding in 1668 of Sault Ste. Marie and St. Mary's Catholic Church.

72 GUT REACTION

How did a nineteenth-century gunshot wound lead to a breakthrough medical discovery?

June 6, 1822, was an ordinary day at John Jacob Astor's American Fur Company Store on Mackinac Island, when suddenly, a shot rang out from a group of young men. French Canadian voyageur Alexis St. Martin was accidentally struck in the stomach at close range—about three feet. Fort Mackinac surgeon Dr. William Beaumont rushed to treat the large wound, which had entered through St. Martin's side and ripped a hole in his stomach. Although Beaumont was able to keep the injured man alive, his efforts to help the gaping wound completely heal were futile.

At age twenty, St. Martin was left with a hole in his stomach and was unable to return to work. While this was distressing for the patient, the doctor saw an opportunity to study the human digestive system. With just a year or two of medical training, Beaumont tapped his curiosity, and with support from colleagues, he began to conduct experiments on St. Martin. Through the hole, the doctor would drop food on a string and periodically retrieve it for observation. With St. Martin working for Beaumont as a handyman, the doctor carried on his study for more than a decade. He was able to

DR. BEAUMONT MUSEUM

WHAT Interpretation of the medical studies done on the victim of a gunshot wound through a stomach opening that wouldn't heal

WHERE Market St., Mackinac Island

COST Adults, $13.50; youth, $8; four and under, free

PRO TIP Admission to Fort Mackinac includes entry to this museum and two additional Historic Downtown Mackinac sites; Biddle House and Mackinac Island Native American Museum; and Richard & Jane Manoogian Mackinac Art Museum.

The American Fur Company Store, stocked with goods, interprets commerce of the era, and hands-on exhibits describe the St. Martin shooting and Beaumont's medical experiments. Photo courtesy of Mackinac Historic State Parks.

conclude that digestion was not a mechanical process, as some had argued, but a chemical process induced by gastric juice. After publishing his findings, he became known as the "Father of Gastric Physiology."

Dr. William Beaumont died in 1853 and has multiple medical facilities named after him in the Detroit area. Alexis St. Martin lived until 1880; his wound never healed.

73 PACK YOUR PARASOL AND BOATER

Wondering where you can escape for a weekend to indulge your inner Victorian?

Hollywood came to Mackinac Island in 1979 and produced the time-travel romance *Somewhere in Time* starring Christopher Reeve and Jane Seymour. Although it tanked at the box office when it was released in 1980, the movie found an audience via video, and it thrives as a cult classic for romantics enchanted by the love story between 1970s playwright Richard Collier (Reeve) and 1912 actress Elise McKenna (Seymour). Mackinac Island, with its Victorian-era architecture and reliance on horses, carriages, and bicycles for transportation, was the ideal setting for the story, based on the book *Bid Time Return* by Richard Matheson.

Each October, hundreds of fans dressed in Victorian (or close enough) garb gather for the Somewhere in Time Weekend at Grand Hotel, the backdrop for the tearjerker. Filming took place at multiple locations on the island, and a walking tour of the sites is a highlight of the annual event. One stop, identified by a plaque as the "Is it You?" spot, is conveniently located on M-185, the eight-mile road that circles the island. The waterside location is the scene of countless reenactments of the first meeting between Richard and Elise, who utter the immortal lines: (Elise) "Is it you?" (Richard) "Yes." Much of the filming took place on the soundstage at

---

Although Mackinac Island banned motor vehicles in 1898, an exception was made for the movie, and Richard was allowed to drive a convertible to Grand Hotel.

Top: Fans dress in elaborate Victorian style for the annual Somewhere in Time *Weekend at Grand Hotel. Photo courtesy of Grand Hotel.*

Inset: No two of Grand Hotel's 397 rooms or suites are alike. This one is decorated in the Somewhere in Time *theme. Photo courtesy of Grand Hotel.*

Mission Point Resort, which at the time was Mackinac College. You can catch a movie at the Mission Point Theater, where a small plaque identifies the seat where Richard sat as he watched Elise on stage.

SOMEWHERE IN TIME WEEKEND

WHAT Annual gathering of fans of the romance movie, who dress in period garb and visit film locations on Mackinac Island

WHERE Grand Hotel, Mackinac Island

COST The two-night packages start at about $1,284 per couple, $1,134 single, and include lodging, meals, film screening, receptions, and costume promenade.

PRO TIP You can conduct a self-guided tour of movie locations at any time—Victorian dress optional. (Non-hotel guests pay a ten-dollar fee to visit Grand Hotel and grounds.)

74 ANIMAL ATTRACTION

Downsizing your taxidermy collection and wondering where can you swap your stuffed squirrel for a beer?

The Bucket of Blood Saloon had been slinging drinks for Sault Ste. Marie patrons from the early 1900s until Prohibition, when it became an incredibly profitable ice cream parlor. The Feds, however, grew suspicious of books that showed nine hundred dollars in profit on a single quart of ice cream.

In 1948 new owners—two Detroit cops—transformed the joint into a bar and restaurant called The Antlers and began filling the rustic space with mounted racks—deer, moose, antelope—and hunters' trophies. Now, more than three hundred critters crowd the walls, ceiling, and rafters, and you'll dine under the steady stare of beavers, ducks, lions, a polar bear, two-headed calf, buffalo, wild boar, giant snake, and fish—including one covered in white fur.

THE ANTLERS

WHAT Good food in a rustic setting filled with stuffed animals

WHERE 804 E. Portage Ave., Sault Ste. Marie

COST Free to gaze at the stuffed menagerie; sandwiches and entrées from about $10 to $20

PRO TIP Vegetarians may want to think twice about dining here.

The bells and whistles that sound in salute to special guests or occasions are a holdover from Prohibition, when they were rung as a warning that the police were coming.

Yes, that's a two-headed calf on the left. Inset: You'll never dine alone at The Antlers.

Owner Chris Szabo calls it a "taxidermy orphanage," and he carries on the tavern's long tradition of bartering a beaver or a bear for a beverage, burger, or more, depending on the size of the specimen up for trade.

Meals are hearty, like the one-pound Paul Bunyan burger or a house specialty, a platter of poutine—twice-fried potatoes mixed with white and orange Wisconsin cheese curds, covered with homemade gravy—served with a slab of venison meatloaf.

75 MYTH INFORMATION

What's more interesting: the story or the repository?

In 1896 in a farmer's field in Newberry, two guys—either woodsmen or hunters—uncover a mysterious stone tablet tangled in the roots of a tree. The stone, measuring nineteen by twenty-six inches, is divided into 140 squares, each one bearing a strange scribble or hieroglyphic. Eureka! Found with it are three small clay figures: a child, a female, and a male. The discovery, as anyone would imagine, causes quite a stir. Speculation runs wild. Did the find date to the Bronze Age, from the Hittite-Minoan culture of two thousand years earlier? Did the writing offer instructions on gaining favor and good luck from the gods, or was it a description of how birds ate grain, or maybe it was a ledger for ancient copper miners? Did the Smithsonian hedge on its initial assessment of the Newberry Tablet as a hoax?

One uncontested aspect of the story seems to be that after the Smithsonian judgment, the farmer tossed the artifacts

NEWBERRY TABLET

WHAT Mysterious etched stone discovered in 1896, described at the Fort de Buade Museum

WHERE 334 N. State St., St. Ignace

COST Free; donations accepted

PRO TIP The museum gift shop carries handcrafted items and prints of historic images in its McKenney and Hall Gallery.

The museum is in the process of relocating, expanding, and reopening as the Straits Cultural Center, also on State Street.

This photo is of a replica of the Newberry Tablet commissioned in recent years by a Newberry business owner.

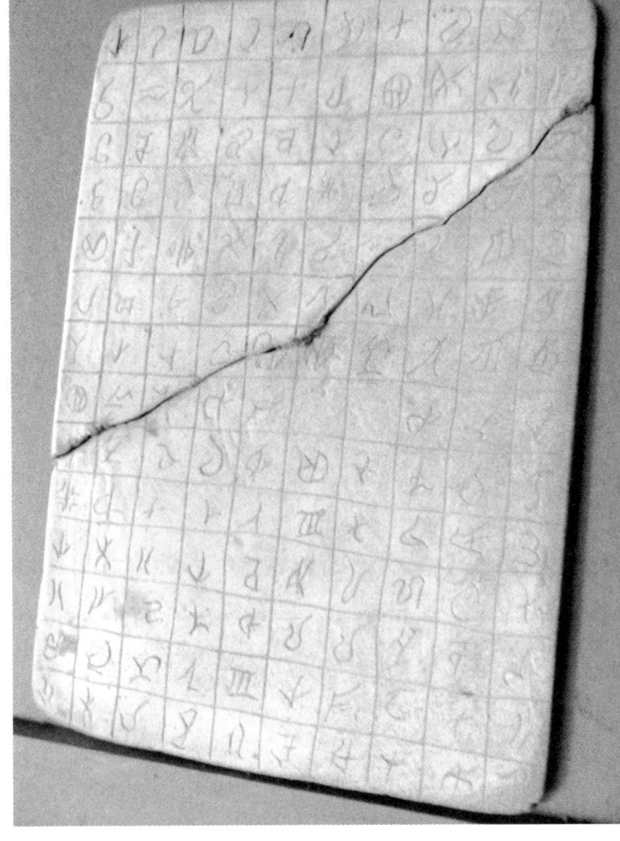

into his barn, where they deteriorated. The pieces eventually ended up in the collection of the Fort de Buade Museum in St. Ignace, where there is a small exhibit dedicated to the tale. But it's the story of the museum that is more interesting than the questionable find of 1896. Decades ago, avid "picker" Donald Benson amassed a treasure trove of items related to the history of St. Ignace and Native American culture. He stashed the items, some dating to the 1600s, in the back of his St. Ignace souvenir shop. When he died, the Sault Tribe of Chippewa Indians purchased the hoard and donated it to the city to be managed by the Michilimackinac Historical Society. It was curated into a fine local history museum named for the French fort located at the spot from 1683 to 1701.

76 BARREL OF FUN

Who vacationed in this teeny cottage?

Long before the current tiny house craze, cartoonist William Donahey and his wife, Mary Dickerson Donahey, a children's book author, spent summers in a bitty bungalow on Grand Sable Lake near Grand Marais. The Pickle Barrel House was inspired by Donahey's popular comic strip *The Teenie Weenies*, which first ran in the *Chicago Tribune* in 1914 and appeared on and off until 1970. The wildly popular comic followed the adventures of two-inch-tall characters dealing with life in a world sized for humans. Donahey's brilliantly hand-colored illustrations depict, in captivating detail, the busy cast of Teenies attempting a daring rescue of a child stranded in a pool-sized cereal bowl or coming home to find a massive mouse asleep in a bed.

In addition to the 2,100 strips he drew for the internationally syndicated feature, Donahey created Teenie Weenie books and put the gang to work in advertisements and product labels for Reid, Murdoch & Company. One of those featured the industrious crew building Monarch Teenie Weenies Sweets pickle kegs, and in 1926 the company had a life-size version built as the Donahey's UP getaway. The sixteen-foot-tall main barrel contains living space on the first floor, with the bedroom up a spiral staircase. The kitchen is in an adjoining eight-foot-tall barrel.

After a decade of dealing with throngs of curiosity seekers, the Donaheys gave up the cottage and it was moved to Grand

---

On the Donaheys' first trip to their new cottage, local children dressed as Teenie Weenies and presented them with the key to their pickle barrel house.

William and Mary Donahey were inspired to create while summering at their unusual cottage on Grand Sable Lake, which is now part of Pictured Rocks National Lakeshore.

Marais, where it served as an information booth and souvenir and ice cream stand. By 2003 the structure was in a state of near collapse. The Grand Marais Historical Society acquired and restored it as a museum, with furnishings and artifacts that depict the period when the Donaheys relaxed and worked there.

PICKLE BARREL HOUSE

WHAT The summer cottage built for a cartoonist to resemble the pickle barrel homes of his tiny characters

WHERE At Randolph St. and Lake Ave., Grand Marais

COST Free; donations accepted

PRO TIP The heirloom irises in the display garden represent different periods of the Pickle Barrel's history. Normal bloom season is late May to late June.

77 KARST QUEST

Where can you go spelunking in a ghost town?

Caves are not among the natural wonders that Michigan is known for, but there is an eerily fascinating landscape with earth cracks, sinkholes, and even a cave to explore at the Fiborn Karst Preserve in the Eastern UP. The word *karst* comes from a Slovene description of a limestone plateau region in southeast Europe. In karst terrain, water runs off the limestone, dolomite, or gypsum surface, and underground drainage dissolves the soluble rock, causing its collapse and sometimes creating dramatic geological formations and disappearing streams. Karst areas in northern Michigan, a part of the Niagara Escarpment, are ringed with limestone and dolomite, which has been quarried in several locations for more than a century. The Fiborn Quarry near Trout Lake yielded a high-calcium limestone from 1905 to 1936 and once was the site of a small town that supported the operation.

The Michigan Karst Conservancy acquired the 480-acre property in 1987. Open to the public to explore on foot, the conservancy includes two self-guided trails that loop past natural landforms and the remains of the small company

FIBORN KARST PRESERVE

WHAT Explore the natural geological formations and ghost town at the former Fiborn Quarry.

WHERE West of Trout Lake, it's a challenge to reach: Take H-40 (Trout Lake Rd.) about eight miles west of the M-123 intersection to Fiborn Quarry Rd. and follow the gravel road north

COST Free; donation to Michigan Karst Conservancy appreciated

PRO TIP Cave passages can be narrow, rough, dark, and wet; appropriate clothing, gloves, footwear, and lighted helmet are required.

The unique natural and historical features of the Fiborn Quarry are protected by the Michigan Karst Conservancy. Photo courtesy of Michigan Karst Conservancy.

town's foundations and structures, including the powerhouse. A highlight is the largest of at least five caves on the property, the approximately 1,500-foot-long Hendrie River Water Cave. Advance permission is required before exploring the cave, and because it's home to the little brown bat and northern long-eared bat, the cave is closed to visitors from mid-October to mid-May. Consult the Michigan Karst Conservancy website for trail guides, rules and guidelines, and permissions required for climbing, specimen collecting, and caving.

Arrange in advance to tour the cave through the Conservancy or on a guided trip by Woods & Waters of Hessel.

78 CRUISING CLASSICS

Where can you find mahogany eye candy bobbing in the water at a premier classic boat show?

At the eastern end of the UP, Les Cheneaux (French for "the channels") is a Lake Huron archipelago of thirty-six islands anchored by the laid-back mainland villages of Hessel and Cedarville. Island cottages are accessible only by boat, and from 1900 through the 1930s, the watercraft of choice was often the now-prized wooden beauties built by Gar Wood and Chris-Craft. In fact, in 1925 EJ Mertaugh Boat Works became the first Chris-Craft franchise in the world and is still in business at the Hessel waterfront. To honor and appreciate the Les Cheneaux boating tradition, in 1978 a couple of local antique wooden boat owners launched what has become one of the premier events for these vintage vessels.

Each August the in-water show attracts about 150 wooden dinghies, rowboats, canoes, sailboats, and runabouts of many makes from across the country. It's fun to walk through the Hessel marina and pick out the sleek, gleaming boat worthy of your Lotto winnings, browse the juried art show, enjoy the live music, and experience the islands on a Channel Cruise, offered several times a day at additional charge (no, not on a vintage vessel—aboard one of the Mackinac Island ferries).

LES CHENEAUX ANTIQUE AND WOODEN BOAT SHOW

WHAT Prize wooden watercraft on display in a top event of its kind

WHERE Hessel Marina

COST Adults, $8; youth under 12, free

PRO TIP Stick around to watch the parade of woodies motor out after the awards ceremony.

Many owners are available to answer questions about their classic wooden boats. Photo by TJ Kozak.

Inspired by the boating history of Les Cheneaux, in 2006 the Great Lakes Boat Building School opened as a traditional, nine-month program and also offers boat-building workshops to the public.

79 OLD AND ODD

Where can you see one-of-a-kind snow machines and learn about the evolution of snowmobiling?

To earn a spot in the Top of the Lake Snowmobile Museum in Naubinway, a sled must meet two criteria: it must be old and it must be odd. The volunteers behind the nonprofit museum take pride in showcasing one-of-a-kind, limited production, prototype, and other machines selected for their rarity and contributions to the history of snowmobiles. Named for its location at the northernmost point of Lake Michigan, the Top of the Lake museum grew from an idea kicked around at the community's annual antique snowmobile show in 2003.

The first exhibit opened with sixty-two loaners from nine collectors and has grown to more than 185 machines, including a surprise contribution of thirty-three sleds from the J. Armand Bombardier Museum of Ingenuity in Valcourt, Quebec. That gift necessitated an expansion just four years after the museum was built. Exhibits illustrate the evolution of the machines from utility to recreational vehicles, including one of the first "snowmobiles," so named in 1917 by Virgil D. White of New Hampshire. He patented a Model T conversion kit that replaced wheels with treads and skis, useful for mail carriers, doctors, fishermen, and other rural workers. Colorful snowmobiles from the 1960s and 1970s represent the heyday of the sport.

Descriptions accompanying the sleds provide information on the mechanics as well as the stories behind them, like the amusingly named Waywego, one of five made by a guy in the

---

Snowmobile literature, ads, promotional items, and vintage snow suits, plus a nifty gift shop, round out the museum offerings.

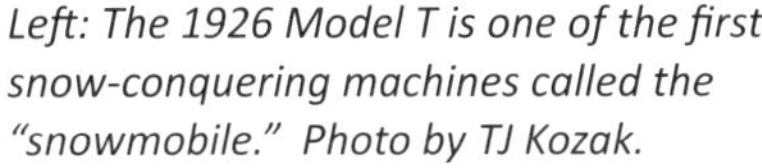

Left: The 1926 Model T is one of the first snow-conquering machines called the "snowmobile." Photo by TJ Kozak.

Top and above right: The museum takes pride in showcasing "old and odd" snowmobile machines.

TOP OF THE LAKE SNOWMOBILE MUSEUM

WHAT Snow machines, gear, and memorabilia that tell the history of snowmobiling.

WHERE W11660 US 2, Naubinway

COST $5; kids, free

PRO TIP The museum hosts several events each year, including the Antique & Vintage Snowmobile Show and Ride in February.

UP town of Trenary. In 1936 Fred Westendorf constructed a boxy, silver metal machine (dubbed the "pizza oven") to take him ice fishing on the Saginaw River. The airsled built in the 1950s in Ely, Minnesota, has a military-grade engine that could reach 100 mph for urgent mail and grocery deliveries. Just ask and knowledgeable museum volunteers offer informal tours, answer questions, and share anecdotes about their passion.

80 YOOPER ZOO

Why does a camel live in the UP woods?

The only moose at GarLyn Zoo was an after-hours visitor who left tracks as it roamed through the property to reach Lake Michigan across the highway. But the UP wildlife park is home to hundreds of other animals found in the north woods, as well as familiar farm critters and exotic species from around the world. The surprising roadside attraction was the dream of Gary and Lynn Moore, who were living in Michigan's Thumb with their kids and a growing domestic pet population when they decided to combine their love of the UP with their love of animals. In 1993, the couple packed up their family—along with their pygmy goats, potbellied pigs, peacocks, and some other animals that don't start with a *p*—and moved to this spot six miles east of Naubinway.

GARLYN ZOO WILDLIFE PARK

WHAT Family-owned and -operated zoo at the northernmost point of Lake Michigan

WHERE W9104 US 2, Naubinway

COST Adults, $15; youth, $7.50; family (up to six), $45

PRO TIP Find quality wildlife-related gifts and typical souvenirs in the gift shop, which also sells feed for the deer, goats, and alpacas and apples for the Syrian bear.

They went about clearing the forest, creating mulch-lined paths, and constructing sturdy animal enclosures, a barn, gift shop, and the garage that for six years they called home. In their second winter, they had to sell their pickup truck to pay the bills. By season three, they started to see their vision realized. Now GarLyn's population includes that camel, plus reindeer, Siberian tigers, sika deer, bobcats, cougars, river otters, African lions, foxes, wolves, tortoises, singing dogs, and a Syrian brown bear, the smallest

Reindeer roam the northwoods setting of GarLyn Zoo, a family-owned and -operated wildlife park that occupies about one-third of its thirty-three-acre property.

member of the grizzly family. In time for the zoo's twenty-fifth anniversary, they added a tropical building for their alligators and other reptiles, monkeys, ring-tailed lemurs, and sloths. GarLyn gets rave reviews for its park-like, family-friendly atmosphere, the close proximity it allows to the animals, and the setting in the woods—visitors have spotted free-roaming coyotes, bobcats, deer, and a wolf on the short drive between the zoo entrance at the highway and the parking lot. Keep an eye out for that moose.

GarLyn Zoo is located at the northernmost point of Lake Michigan, forty minutes west of the Mackinac Bridge along US 2, a designated scenic Pure Michigan Byway.

81 BURGER WARS

Do you want a bridge, ferry, or fries with that?

How many places are lucky enough to have not one, but a choice of two, classic drive-ins, located just about three miles apart? In Sault Ste. Marie, loyalties are divided between Clyde's Drive-In on the eastern end of Riverside Drive and West Pier Drive-In on, well, the west side of town. Both spots have indoor seating—just a handful of counter stools—but the appeal of old-fashioned joints like these is the nostalgia of a carhop taking your order and delivering it on a tray that hangs on the vehicle window. Menus are familiar: burgers, fries, shakes, malts, and deep-fried vegetables. Sure, there are BLTs and fish sandwiches, etc., but this is about burgers. Both drive-ins usually end up going bun-to-bun in every Best Burger competition in the UP—often statewide, too. Both serve up thick, not-too-juicy patties that don't fall apart. Fries are crinkle cut at West Pier, traditional at Clyde's, and both emerge from the fryer crispy outside, just right inside. Chocolate malts at both are thick and tasty.

CLYDE'S DRIVE-IN VS. WEST PIER DRIVE-IN

WHAT Classic drive-ins located just three miles apart, complete with carhops delivering award-winning burgers and the works

WHERE Clyde's: 1425 Riverside Dr., Sault Ste. Marie | West Pier Drive-In: 849 W. Pier Dr., Sault Ste. Marie

COST Cheeseburger, $5 to $10, depending on size; French fries, $2.50; chocolate malt, $2.75

PRO TIP Add an order of deep-fried cauliflower at Clyde's, onion rings at West Pier.

There's a seasonal Clyde's in St. Ignace and a year-round location in Manistique.

Top left: The mantra at the tiny West Pier is "No frills, no debit or credit cards." Photo by TJ Kozak.

Above left: Clyde's was founded in 1949 by Clyde VanDusen, who still owns the drive-in. Photo by TJ Kozak.

Right: Clyde's and West Pier each have legions of fans who taste a difference between the thick, moist burgers at the authentic drive-ins.

Service is friendly but no-frills. Prices are competitive. West Pier is cash only, so if you're low on dough, go to Clyde's, where cards are accepted. The tiebreaker may be the locale. Both are on the water with views of passing freighters. The West Pier is in the shadow of the 2.8-mile International Bridge and the vertical lift rail bridge; they span the Saint Marys River and Soo Locks to connect the U.S. and Canadian Sault Ste. Maries. At Clyde's, the show is the Sugar Island ferry as it loads, unloads, and shuttles vehicles and passengers back and forth.

Need another tiebreaker? You can satisfy your burger craving at 9 a.m. at Clyde's; West Pier doesn't open until 11.

82 FUR FORTUNE

Who is the illiterate female fur trader who gave John Jacob Astor a run for his money?

One of the most successful nineteenth-century businesswomen in the country's Northwest Territory was Magdelaine La Framboise, who lived out her final years in a lovely Mackinac Island home that she built with the fortune she made in the fur trade. Born in 1780 to a French-Canadian father and an Ottawa mother, at the age of fourteen Magdelaine married fur trader Joseph La Framboise and joined him in his business. They traveled seasonally between their trading post in Michigan's southwest Lower Peninsula and Mackinac Island, and it was on one of these trips, in 1806, that Joseph was murdered. Magdelaine, with two children to support, returned to Mackinac Island and carried on and expanded the fur operation.

MAGDELAINE LA FRAMBOISE GRAVESITE

WHAT Resting place of a woman important in Mackinac Island history, located on the grounds of Ste. Anne Catholic Church.

WHERE 6836 Huron Rd., Mackinac Island

COST Free entry

PRO TIP You can stay overnight at Madame's Chateau La Framboise, the centerpiece of the Harbour View Inn lodging compound.

Although she spoke four languages (French, English, Ottawa, and Chippewa), La Framboise couldn't read or write. Still, she was a formidable competitor for John Jacob Astor, who established his American Fur Company on Mackinac Island in 1808. By 1818 Astor's company had made her an offer she couldn't refuse, and La Framboise sold her business. She retired a wealthy woman and in 1822 built the elegant Chateau La Framboise on Mackinac

Left: Mackinac Island's Ste. Anne Catholic Church was built on land donated by Magdelaine La Framboise.

Right: Magdelaine La Framboise is buried with her beloved daughter on the grounds of Ste. Anne Catholic Church on Mackinac Island.

Island. She learned to read and write and dedicated her attention to the Catholic church and the education of the island's Native American children. Her son, Joseph La Framboise, became a fur trader in Canada and Minnesota, and her daughter, Josephine, married Benjamin Kendrick Pierce, commander of Fort Mackinac and brother of President Franklin Pierce.

La Framboise, who died in 1846, donated property adjacent to her home for Ste. Anne Catholic Church. It is still an active parish and houses a museum about the religious history of the island. She and her daughter and granddaughter are buried on the church grounds.

Magdelaine La Framboise, the most prominent of Mackinac Island's métis (French and American Indian) women, was described as tall and dignified and was known for wearing her native dress throughout her life.

83 THEY HAVE A LOCK ON IT

Where in the world can you ride through a stupendous nautical locking system?

Granted, it's not something that many people consider on a daily basis. But for centuries, the Great Lakes have played an important part in the world economy. The UP is surrounded by three of the five greatest freshwater seas on the planet: the Great Lakes Michigan, Huron, and Superior. For centuries, these waters have been plied by Native Americans, voyageurs, missionaries, fur traders, mining and logging companies, and other merchants—and, since 1934, the Soo Locks Boat Tours. The private company takes boatloads of visitors through the engineering marvel that allows navigation of the twenty-one-foot drop between Lakes Superior and Huron at the international border between the twin cities of Sault Ste. Marie, Michigan, and Sault Ste. Marie, Ontario, Canada.

SOO LOCKS BOAT TOURS

WHAT Experience "locking through" the engineering marvel and get an up-close look at the operation, sometimes alongside massive lake and ocean freighters, on a two-hour boat tour.

WHERE Two dock locations on Portage Ave., Sault Ste. Marie

COST Adults, $33; youth, $12; under five, free

PRO TIP Check the boat schedule hotline at 906-253-9290 to see when freighters will be locking through.

Initially, canoes and boats were portaged around the St. Marys Rapids between the lakes, but as industry and boats grew, the solution was to build a lock that allowed vessels to be raised and lowered to meet the different water levels. The first lock, built in 1798, was destroyed during the War of 1812. A series of locks was constructed from 1855 to 1919

Watch boats move through the passage from the observation platform at the free Soo Locks Visitor Center.

to accommodate the bigger boats and busy traffic. The US Army Corps of Engineers is responsible for the two locks currently in use, the MacArthur, which opened in 1943, and the Poe, built in 1968 to handle one-thousand-foot freighters. At the free Soo Locks Visitor Center, exhibits describe the system of gates, gravity, and valves that controls water depths to lift and lower boats to lake levels, and you can watch boats "lock through" from an elevated platform.

The Soo locks handle an average of seven thousand vessels and eighty million tons of cargo in each ten-month season.

84 GRAVE CONCERN

Is Father Marquette's final resting place really final?

Spend any time in the UP and it becomes obvious that Father Jacques Marquette was an important figure, given the multiple statues and, of course, its largest city and county, which are named for the missionary and explorer. Jacques Marquette was born in France on June 1, 1637, and at age seventeen joined the Society of Jesus. In 1666 he was sent to New France as a missionary, and after two years he traveled west to the UP, where he established Michigan's first European settlements: Sault Ste. Marie in 1668 and St. Ignace in 1671. It is in St. Ignace that he is buried. Perhaps.

In May of 1673 Father Marquette and Louis Jolliet launched an expedition to explore and map the Mississippi River. On their return north, Marquette became ill with dysentery and died in May of 1675 along the Lower Peninsula's Lake Michigan shore. He was buried near what is now Ludington. In 1677 Marquette's remains were taken to St. Ignace for interment at the mission he'd established. It remained an active mission until about 1705, when it was abandoned and burned, its location forgotten. By the 1830s, a new mission was established at St. Ignace. In 1877, during an excavation, evidence of the original site was uncovered, including what was left of Father Marquette. A 1972 dig led by Dr. Lyle M. Stone, staff archaeologist for the Mackinac Island State Park Commission, concluded that it was, probably, the correct site. According to a story in *The Detroit News*, Dr. Stone said, "We'll never find a bronze plaque saying, 'Here lies Fr. Marquette,' but this is the only active candidate we have at this time."

A statue of Marquette stands in a garden next to the Museum of Ojibwa Culture, where a monument dedicated by the city in 1882 marks the priest's final resting place.

FATHER MARQUETTE MISSION PARK

WHAT Burial site of Father Jacques Marquette

WHERE 500 N. State St., St. Ignace

COST Free; donations accepted

PRO TIP Enjoy views of the Mackinac Bridge from the Father Marquette National Memorial nearby at Straits State Park in St. Ignace.

One of three UP sculptures of Father Marquette stands over his gravesite on the grounds of the mission he founded in St. Ignace.

There are three statues to Father Marquette across the UP. In addition to St. Ignace, he stands in Marquette Park on Mackinac Island and overlooks his namesake city of Marquette.

85 SISU SISTER

What woman established a utopian community for Finnish immigrants in the UP?

Finnish people have a word, *sisu*, for what can be summed up as determination, perseverance, and grit. One woman who was known across the UP, from Calumet to Drummond Island, personified *sisu*. Born in Tornio, Finland, in 1861, Margareeta Johanna Konttra Niiranen came to the United States at the age of twenty and changed her name to Maggie Walz. By day she worked as a domestic for a family in the Houghton area, and at night she learned English. She sold items door to door and worked as a salesclerk at a department store.

KREETAN

WHAT Site of an early-twentieth-century Finnish colony on Drummond Island

WHERE South shore, in the area of Scammon Cove

COST Free

PRO TIP The Drummond Island Historical Museum has an exhibit on the Finnish community established by Maggie Walz.

Walz made trips to Finland to bring young women to the UP, where she helped them assimilate to America. After earning a business degree at Valparaiso College in Indiana, she settled in Calumet, created a Finnish women's society that presented thought-provoking programs, and published a newspaper. She established herself as a businesswoman and built a large, commercial building in Calumet. In 1903, as a land agent, Walz envisioned a utopian community on homesteading land on Drummond Island, where Finnish immigrants would live cooperative, self-sufficient lives according to the ideals of Christianity and temperance. In 1905, she and twenty-five others, chosen for the diverse skills needed to establish the settlement, traveled to Drummond

Only the Finnish road names hint at the location of the experimental colony, but there's a nice park at Scammon Bay to sit and reflect on the effort. Portrait photo courtesy of Keweenaw National Historical Park.

Island. They farmed the poor, rocky land and set up a logging and lumber operation, post office, school, and general store. Within five years, the colony, named Kreetan, had grown to a population of about 205. They built a Finn Hall for socializing. "Worldly" pursuits began chipping away at the colony's founding ideals.

By 1914 Walz, who had been commuting between Calumet and Kreetan, gave up on the community and turned her attention to suffrage, temperance, and social welfare interests. She died in 1927, and in 2015 she was inducted into the Michigan Women's Hall of Fame.

The town name of Kreetan was derived from Maggie Walz's name Margareeta (Kreeta).

86 POETRY IN MOTION

What are the rushing waters that Longfellow wrote about?

In his 1855 epic poem *The Song of Hiawatha*, Henry Wadsworth Longfellow tells the tale of an Ojibwa named Hiawatha and his love for Minnehaha. The setting is the south shore of Gitche Gumee—Lake Superior—at the Pictured Rocks in the UP.

By the shores of Gitche Gumee,
By the shining Big-Sea-Water,
Stood the wigwam of Nokomis,
Daughter of the Moon, Nokomis.

Some of the story takes place at Taquamenaw, now known as the Tahquamenon River and Falls. Of Michigan's two hundred named waterfalls, the largest, likely the most photographed, and best known are the Upper Falls at the forty-six-thousand-acre Tahquamenon Falls State Park, west of the Lake Superior village of Paradise. This is the more dramatic and larger of two falls on the Tahquamenon River. At the two-hundred-foot-wide Upper Falls, the root beer-colored water rushes over the nearly fifty-foot drop at an average of five thousand gallons per second (although during peak times the flow can be up to ten times that). The brown hue of the water is due to the tannic acid seeping from surrounding cedar, hemlock, and spruce trees. There are accessible viewing areas overlooking the falls, as well as two platforms requiring descent (and the return climb up) of about one hundred steps each.

A short drive or a four-mile hike through the woods connects the Upper to the lesser known Lower Falls, where the experience is completely different. The series of five cascades that gradually step down twenty-two feet are more approachable, serene, and at the same time playful. Here, you can wade in the water and rent a rowboat to explore the river and head to the island that sits in the middle of the falls. The island's half-mile loop walking trail takes you right next to the rushing waters.

There's a dramatic difference between the tall, wide, and majestic Upper Tahquamenon Falls and the stepped, more approachable Lower Falls.

TAHQUAMENON FALLS

WHAT The Upper and Lower Falls of the Tahquamenon River

WHERE Entrances are off M-123, west of Paradise

COST Recreation Passport required: residents, $12 annual; non-residents, $9 day pass, $34 annual. Boat rentals per person, $7; family (up to six people), $20

PRO TIP Summer days can be very crowded; don't overlook an early September visit, when the weather and water can still be warm. Fall colors and the snowy winter scenery are both spectacular.

"Lay aside your cloak, O Birch-tree!
Lay aside your white-skin wrapper,
For the Summer-time is coming,
And the sun is warm in heaven,
And you need no white-skin wrapper!"
Thus aloud cried Hiawatha
In the solitary forest,
By the rushing Taquamenaw…

87 STORYBOOK COTTAGE

Where can you buy used and rare books in a quaint 1920s cabin?

Once upon a time, Mary Carney had a bookstore named First Edition in the Lower Peninsula city of Muskegon. But there came a day—oh, just a few years ago—that Mary remembers with a laugh: "I just had to run away" to the UP. So, she put Michigan's Mitten in her rearview mirror and headed north, across the Mackinac Bridge.

Carney ended up at a spot called Brevort, at a property tucked away off the main highway. "I found this poor old place that was just hanging around. There were four cabins." She made herself at home in the late-1800s mail stage stop and looked at the empty cabins, which had been built in 1921, and did not say to herself, "I will open a bookstore." But after a while she thought, "Well, I'll just bring some books up from the store in Muskegon . . . "

The shop below the Big Mac Bridge is long gone, but after thirty-three years the First Edition, Too Bookstore is still open, by chance or by appointment. If Carney is out "chasing down books," her husband Warren Cunningham may be there to open the shop for the avid collectors and other booklovers who seek and find the five-room cabin filled with new, used, and rare books.

"The specialty of the house is Michigan history, and Great Lakes history," Carney says, though she does carry some fiction, gardening, crafts, natural history, and other topics among the seventy-five thousand books in stock. "Diehard

---

Mary Carney says the by chance or by appointment shop hours work for her and the following she's built up in her forty-five years of selling books.

The circa-1920s book-filled cabin and flower garden invite lingering.

collectors have followed me here," coming many miles from the Mitten below the big bridge and beyond. If you can't make it to the bookstore, check the online inventory or contact her through the website for further help with a search.

FIRST EDITION, TOO BOOKSTORE

WHAT Cozy bookshop in the woods

WHERE 461 Worth Rd. at the corner of Schoolhouse Rd. a half-mile off US 2, Brevort

COST Free to browse, but you'll end up buying something!

PRO TIP Set a spell and read in Mary's flower garden filled with whimsical yard art.

88 RARE EARTH

Where can you explore a variety of unique and scenic geological features on one island?

Drummond Island, one of the largest islands in the Great Lakes, is located at the far Eastern UP and is accessible year-round by a one-mile car ferry ride from De Tour Village. The state owns more than half of its eighty-seven thousand acres, which are thickly wooded and dotted with thirty-four lakes. The Lake Huron island is geologically interesting because of its unusual land formations, and it is one of only a few places to find the speckled Jasper conglomerate. The distinctive quartz and pebble rock was named puddingstone by the British because they thought it looked like boiled suet pudding with berries.

DRUMMOND ISLAND

WHAT Unique land features on one of the largest islands in the Great Lakes

WHERE Multiple sites on Drummond Island

COST Free, after ferry fare to island ($14 roundtrip for vehicle and driver)

PRO TIP If you don't have luck on your puddingstone hunt, head to North Haven Gift Shop for jewelry and home decor items made on site.

Drummond is home to a globally rare ecosystem known as an alvar, a limestone plain with little soil, which, outside the Great Lakes region, is found only in Sweden, Estonia, England, and Ireland. The flat, exposed bedrock looks like sections of pavement, and only select plants are able to survive. The Nature Conservancy protects 1,210 acres as the Maxton Plains Preserve, which it classifies as the largest high-quality alvar in North America. Wildflowers and grasses include prairie smoke, Indian paintbrush, and prairie dropseed, and many species of rare and threatened birds are attracted to the environment.

Left: Drummond Island is one of the few places that puddingstone is found.

Right: The Maxton Plains Preserve is home to North America's largest high-quality alvar.

Some of Drummond's unique, natural attractions are accessible only by four-wheel drive vehicle, mountain biking, or hiking. It's a rugged but worthwhile drive to the Fossil Ledges, remnants of an ancient salt water coral bed on the north shore of the island. The view from the cliff at Marble Head, at the easternmost point in the UP, and a series of broad rock shelves called the Steps at Marble Head, make this a popular destination for off-roaders. Get detailed driving instructions and trail conditions from the visitor information center.

Drummond Island is part of an archipelago of fifty-six islands, and some of its beauty is best appreciated from the water. The Fossil Ledges and Marble Head are two of the top paddling destinations along the 150-mile shoreline.

89 MUDDYING THE WATERS

How did The Snows become known for Jersey Mud?

The community of thirty-six Les Cheneaux Islands in the Eastern UP, anchored by the mainland villages of Hessel and Cedarville, has been a popular Lake Huron resort area since the late 1800s. French for "the channels," it is pronounced lay-she-NO, and nicknamed The Snows. For generations of residents and visitors, there's one treat synonymous with The Snows: Jersey Mud, a concoction that was the specialty of Cedarville's popular Bon-Air ice cream parlor. When Jill and Jeff McLeod opened their Ice Cream Shoppe fifteen years ago, the Bon-Air owners shared the scoop on how the century-old sweet came to The Snows.

The framed, undated letter from B. Clarke Morse Jr. of St. Ledger Island in Hessel explains:

In May of 1920 Katherine Miller and I were married and we spent one week of our honeymoon in New York City. While there we were introduced to the JERSEY MUD.

THE ICE CREAM SHOPPE

WHAT Jersey Mud, an ice cream treat special to Les Cheneaux

WHERE 38 E. Hodeck St., Cedarville

COST Pick your portion: $4, $4.50, $5

PRO TIP Time your visit to compete in the July 4th Jersey Mud Eating Contest.

The Ice Cream Shoppe serves its Jersey Mud as a sundae, with a cherry on top.

A homemade version of the century-old treat, before being stirred and turned to mud. Photo by TJ Kozak.

Later that summer we visited Katherine's family at the Les Cheneaux Club. Of course we had to go and see our friend George LeFleur of the Bon Air. George wanted to know what was new in New York and we told him about the Jersey Mud. Right off the bat George wanted to know how it was made.

THIS IS HOW

Into a tall soda glass one shot of chocolate sauce, then one scoop of vanilla ice cream, another shot of chocolate sauce, one more scoop of vanilla ice cream, topped with a heaping tablespoon of malted milk. With a long spoon start stirring until it has the consistency of mud. Then start eating. If you like marshmallow on top that is fine. It was not on the original.

INDEX